FE
NC
E

Fence Volume 18, Number 2
©2017 Fence Magazine, Incorporated

Front cover: *Foster as Maxe (for The Husbands)* by Buzz Slutzky. 2017. 9 1/2" x 7.5", ink on vellum.
Back cover: *Hot Tub Embrace (for The Husbands)* by Buzz Slutzky. 2017. 7 1/4" x 5 1/2", ink on vellum.

Fence is published biannually, in print, in Spring and Fall.

Fence receives submissions electronically at **fence.submittable.com**. Response time is between three and nine months. Repeat publications take place after at least four issues or two years have elapsed.

Find us at **fenceportal.org** or **fence.fencebooks@gmail.com**.
Or, at (518) 567-7006.

Or, *Fence*
    Science Library 320
    University at Albany
    1400 Washington Avenue
    Albany, NY 12222

This issue of *Fence* was printed in the United States by Versa Press. *Fence* is distributed in North America by: Small Press Distribution, Berkeley, CA (510) 524-1668; and Ubiquity, Brooklyn, NY (718) 875-5491.

ISBN: 978-1-944380-04-5
ISSN: 1097-9980

FENCE is published by Fence Magazine, Incorporated, a not-for-profit corporation in partnership with the University at Albany and the New York State Writers Institute. Donations and gifts are tax-deductible to the extent allowed by law.

Fence is made possible by the generous agency of the Fence Trust and all Friends of *Fence*.

A one-year subscription is $22; two-year subscription is $32. A donation of $300 and more makes the donor a "Friend of *Fence*" and is good for a lifetime subscription. Annual donors at $1,000 or above are members of the Fence Trust.

If you'd like to support *Fence*, please contact Rebecca Wolff at **rebeccafence@gmail.com**.

FENCE

SUMMER 2017

CONTENTS VOL. 18 NO. 2

EDITOR'S NOTE   *Rav Grewal-Kök*   VII

POETRY

CHRIS STROFFOLINO	*Sonnet 12: A Dialogue*	1
RAQUEL GUTIÉRREZ	*#39*	2
JASMINE DREAME WAGNER	*American Pedigree*	3
CALEB NOLEN	*Two poems*	8
TOM HAVIV	*Didactic Poem*	20
URAYOÁN NOEL	*en flor ida*	28
LUCY BURNS	*Almost Gone*	32
KATHRYN MARIS	*Two poems*	48
M. WEST	*Ganzfeld, Los Angeles*	59
NICHOLAS D. NACE	*The Hundred Faults*	61
WILL SMILEY	*Max Pengall's Christmas Story*	77
CARMEN GIMÉNEZ SMITH	*from "Post Identity"*	78
MARTY CAIN	THE VALUES BY WHICH MEN HAVE FOUND IT POSSIBLE NOT MERELY TO SURVIVE BUT TO LIVE WITH DIGNITY	90
ELIZABETH CLARK WESSEL	*Carol and Shirley*	91
KATHERINE A FOWLEY	*Two poems*	106
HANNAH BROOKS-MOTL	*Stanford*	120
EDWIN TORRES	*Lucifer's G-Spot*	121
JULIA TILLINGHAST	*Three poems*	123
HAZEL WHITE	*from "Vigilance Is No Orchard"*	132
RUSTY MORRISON	*Two poems*	134
DANIEL BORZUTZKY	*Two poems*	136
KELLI ANNE NOFTLE	*The Hair*	145
ALIX ANNE SHAW	*Weapons Of*	147
JASON MITCHELL	*good sign*	149
FLORENCE KINDEL	*Late Afternoon*	150

FICTION

OSAMA ALOMAR	*Six stories*	6
HILARY PLUM	*Calque*	10
YANARA FRIEDLAND	*As If Raising A Flag For An Unknown Country That Is One's Own*	16
MARI CHRISTMAS	*Woodland*	34
AARON COLEMAN	*Shadows Uplifted*	50
DAVID GREENWOOD	*A Little Place*	57
GINA ABELKOP	*We Love Venus!*	67
DAVID HOLLANDER	*A Complete Picture*	84
VALÉRIE MRÉJEN	*from "Eau Sauvage"*	110
JENNIFER ADAMS	*Girl on a Balcony*	115
NOY HOLLAND	*Three stories*	129

OTHER

DIANA CAGE	*The Husbands*	92

ART

BUZZ SLUTZKY	*Covers & illustrations*	

READING LIST

	151

RAV GREWAL-KÖK

What Are We Doing Here?

A friend recently told me he hasn't been able to write since the election. Over the past twenty years he has produced novels, stories, journalism, essays, and reviews in what seemed to be a steady stream, but now the whole enterprise seems futile. His head is muddled. He can't begin anything new. Like me, this friend is a dark-skinned immigrant. Trump's victory, fueled in part by white identity politics and racial resentment, swept away my friend's old certainties (or, if not certainties, then dearly-held hopes). In their place, something older—a mix, perhaps, of fear, sadness, and scorn—has returned. I understand where my friend is coming from. Since the election I've lost entire weeks. I don't sleep well. I'm not hiding in my house but now, when I go out at night for a drink, my wife (light-skinned, but also an immigrant, with a Muslim father) tells me to keep my eyes open. I tell her I always do. Both of us are glad we no longer live in Missouri.

Not that you have to be an immigrant. Anyone who is at all concerned about racial justice, women's rights, reproductive rights, queer rights, indigenous rights, the labor movement, anti-Muslim bigotry, the prison-industrial complex, public schools, clean air and water, the climate catastrophe, health care, child care, poverty, hunger, student debt, foreign wars, torture, scientific research, arts funding, or a hundred other causes must recognize that we are living through an emergency. The bad news doesn't stop. Of course, some tens of millions of my fellow citizens may view the present situation differently—just enough of them certainly voted differently—but I don't know anyone who hasn't felt, at various times since the inauguration, soiled, exhausted, and overwhelmed.

What, under these conditions, is the point of a literary magazine? Why write, edit, publish? Why, reader, do you read? Literature is not an instrument. The poems and stories that appear in these pages will not alter the political situation. Time spent with *Fence* is time away from putting your body in the streets, or calling your senator, or raising your middle finger.

I don't have an answer, only another kind of feeling. We fiction editors chose most of the stories for this issue in the late summer and early fall of 2016. Back then I was expecting another outcome. Fool that I was, I only wanted a dispiriting election season to be over. Looking back at these stories now, I can't help but think of how different life seemed a short time ago. But I also remember, when I read Aaron Coleman's rewriting of *Iola Leroy*, that nothing we face is new. And we still have experience, restraint, rhythm, and those blank spaces on the page that take your breath away. "Let the trees go. Let the secrets go. I can't let this skin go. I don't want to bloodlet home, go." What I would still give for an ear like Noy Holland's, who sings of beauty and love right at the edge of the abyss. "Like a beacon, such pain, a knuckle pulsing in the night." Osama Alomar, Syrian immigrant and Exiled Writer-in-Residence at Pittsburgh's City of Asylum, reminds us, like Beckett and Kafka before him, that we can always laugh at our own futility, even as we never turn away from the horror.

In rereading the fiction printed in this issue, I'm not consoled. I just feel more like myself. Aren't all these gestures—reading, writing, editing—also reminders that another life, an intimate life, still exists? I don't think it's escapism to reserve a space for gratitude. I will forget that truth, perhaps as soon as I finish writing this note and look at the day's headlines. So I will have to find a way back to remembering again.

It has been worse. It will get worse. Let's go on.

FENCE could not continue without the collaboration and support of the following individuals, organizations, and institutions. *Fence* thanks you.

ELISA ALBERT & EDWARD SCHWARZSCHILD

MARY JO BANG

BILL CLEGG

ALAN COON & KELLY DRAHUSHUK/
SPOTTY DOG BOOKS & ALE

JENNIFER EPSTEIN

SUSIE GILBERT

BRENDA HILLMAN

MENACHEM KAISER

WILLIAM & DANA KENNEDY

KATY LEDERER & BEN STATZ

JONATHAN LETHEM

NATIONAL ENDOWMENT FOR THE ARTS

NEW YORK STATE COUNCIL ON THE ARTS

GEORGE ROSS

PETER STRAUB

JULIA STRAYER

COLE SWENSEN

LYNNE TILLMAN

ROB WILSON & THE SELECT EQUITY GROUP

THE UNIVERSITY AT ALBANY

Fence Magazine, Inc. welcomes your tax-deductible donations. Because of our non-profit status, Fence is never required by its board to make editorial decisions based on the requirements of any market force or capital concern, but only with reference to its mission and its vision. Please consider joining our list of supporters.

Sonnet 12: A Dialogue

"Do you know that it really could be cool
and hot, if we two could cross-pollinate,
could hug and dance and not be home too late
we could forget the past and start anew."
"I don't mind if youth lead the movement, and
let us steep our old riffs in their new sounds
never as new as they might think, and round
us, to glow a soul we can understand."
"You lost me with youth," "I bet I could be
a kickass step-dad," "You know you must drum
a goofy & humble tune to win me."
"I'll listen and follow." "As long as some
room's left for deep clean oceans, I can come
back I always will." "I love when you hum."

RAQUEL GUTIÉRREZ

#39

Curse the state of contemporary art
Mid-Spring; I sit up front behind Black
Church, an elegant curvature as lithe and
white masculine bodies seize the
season amongst the seizure-inspiring

strobe; when I follow the catwalking
I see the entire audience behind me; angular
asexual. A brutalist movement. And muscle
butch queens are the only semblance of
camp

there is only one black choreographer
and she shouts me down about cunty realness;
scolds the woman in front of me about
her less than ebullient response to her call and
now perhaps less shall travel to Harlem.

Non-existent is the approach.
Is it just
better to not exist?
Question the approach to
the House of Xtravanganza

and other grander
authenticities with custody; even
the highest of priestesses
greet Yemaya with their backs
turned to the ocean

American Pedigree

I have an idea.
It's a bad idea. As always.
It's a bad idea. As always.
I am drawn to my bad ideas.
What makes an idea bad?
Is it the possibility.
Of sincerity turning into nothing.
Is it the horror.
Of possibly actually.
Of closing a window.
Of going outside and hallucinating.
Mallarmé.
Calling the anarchists.
"Angels of Purity"

Red light. One car.
Four-way. Three.
Choices. This town is.
A cancer cluster.
Of common names.

Jennifers Catharines Sarahs
Marys Kristies Sophies

An LED sun.
Shocks.
Night into scaffolding.
 …
  scaffolding
 …
  scaffolding
 …
  scaffolding

The no tree backyards.
The.
Korn Slipknot Wilco
Heathers Jessicas Amandas play.
Sorry.
Sorry.
Sorry.
"Butterfly . . . Sugar . . . Baby"
Fucked.

Up Ford. Fucked.
Acura. Here.
Everybody knows.
Your prodigy sibling.
Even the pigs.
    The pigs.

Marks Pauls Davids
Jims Toms Josephs
Pauls Mikes Matts

No matter.
How or where.
I am the center. *THEY ARE LOOKING*
I am a video game.
Dominatrix. Strapped in.
Black vinyl.
Information. I am.

The prairie macho and.
Severe in my bullshit.
The peacock.
Is the first real thing.
I achieve.

Karens Dorothys Kelleys
Lukes Toms Christies
Frederica Veronica

The sink caught.
The blue dye. Now there is.
A blue eye.
Nothing can touch me.

    ...

   scaffolding

    ...

   scaffolding

    ...

   scaffolding

The Knife

He was born with a silver knife in his mouth. And he was its first victim.

Bowed Heads

An empty ear of wheat looked across the field to a crowd standing in a line along the straight road. Their heads were bent before their tyrant leader. The empty ear said sadly to herself "How lucky are these human ears! Their heads are bowed with the blessing of fullness!"

The Feather and the Wind

The feather said to the wind in a slain voice: "What's this tyranny?"
The wind answered her: "What's this weakness?"

Vision

Because his eyes had microscopic powers it was necessary for him to pass through towering mountains and rugged declivities in the flatlands of his life.

And thus he arrived at his goal very late.

Struggle of Opposites

Nature said, "The world is based on the struggle of opposites." The Tyrant added: "Under my leadership!"

The Teeth of the Comb

Some of the teeth of the comb were envious of the class differences that exist between humans. They strove desperately to increase their height, and, when they succeeded, began to look with disdain on their colleagues below.

After a little while the comb's owner felt a desire to comb his hair. But when found it in this state he threw it in the garbage.

Translations by C.J. Collins.

CALEB NOLEN

Dream with Commentary

with open eyes i swam beneath the surface of a lake and as a fisherman
casts his fishing lines so did the sun cast rays into the shadowed green.
i was alone until i came upon the dead men, a field of them,
each floating at the end of a long chain that descended down to darkness,
like balloons tethered to a child's wrist, their sodden flesh had begun to slip
the way i'm told clothes can slip from the body of someone beautiful
when they choose to undress before you. i cannot remember
what else happened only that i woke lonely wondering
how long a corpse can float before it is overcome.

it is so difficult to love someone, other humans
make such demands and not unjustly, i just can't say no
once feelings start.

The Language of Love

no one can call it objectifying women if you're imagining yourself
as the woman when you're watching porn, if you're j-ing off while
contemplating being held down by someone stronger, made to do
whatever, bend this way suck that cock open this hole and smile.
i could never. i can submit but i need the semblance of control i
need to believe i could push the person off and fuck them up
if they went too far, not just hope they would heed my words.
i do not understand how women sleep with men.

in the bible God says let there be light and there is, He says
come to me and Peter walks on water, He says this is my body broken
for you and the world is redeemed, but human words just dissipate
like steam they don't do anything.

once a man had my ear in his teeth and my ass in his hands. he had
to lean towards me he was so tall and when he asked me to leave
with him i wanted to. i wanted to say you can fuck me as long as
i can hold a knife but it would have been too awkward i went
to the bathroom, my hands were shaking i was so nervous,
i looked in the mirror and mouthed just go home. i ran
my hands under the cold water and found the back door.

Calque

Just last week I received in the mail a copy of my old chapter on Anastasia Calque, with one of my best lines (I had thought at the time) double underlined:

Each story is the story of a marriage, and who is dead in the end.

Well, I had written it; I would write nothing like it now, but what does that matter? I am no longer young and no longer need to mean everything always, like some sort of monk or machine.

My work on Calque and her minor novel *Eyes of the Moth* is still widely cited. The novel had vanished, out of print, long before Calque's death, her death which must now be, it is strange to think, thirty years ago. She had died without heir and her effects were left neglected in her apartment, which a trollish distant cousin or aunt now inhabited. After a decade of unanswered letters, one of Anastasia's former lovers had in frustration shown up at the door, to plead with the aunt for one afternoon to sort and catalog Anastasia's things. There must be letters from her godfather, the lover had persuaded the aunt, and these will be worth something. The godfather was long dead, but his films were now being remastered, and had there been anything more than a few snapshots of him, with his silly signature high-waisted pants, eating ices with the young Calque on a dock, seagulls wheeling, no doubt they would indeed have sold. It was then that the lover had discovered Calque's neat boxes of original manuscripts, among them *Eyes of the Moth*, which she retrieved, the aunt's acquiescence reluctant. Thus seventeen years ago a copy of the novel had appeared in my department mail. Courtesy of this same former lover, whose note to me, in English, said only: *This must be published. E.*

At that time, of Calque's five novels only one had been translated into English—by, it's worth noting, the new husband of the same E, Calque's erstwhile lover. The rest of Calque's work was read ravenously and to some degree canonized in her home country, but never known or wholly forgotten outside it. The rest except for *Eyes of the Moth*, that is, which had never been available anywhere after the first print run was lost to fire. A handful of copies had always been said to have survived the flames, and in the years before E's package arrived I had attempted several times to obtain one, although at least twice I'd paid through the nose for what turned out to be the wrong book—refunds of course, in the unhinged capitalism of that country, impossible.

The fire had been no accident; rather a deliberate attack on the house that published all the great leftist writers of the time. It was the eve of the military coup, and it was never at least to my research definitively clear which of the pathetic right-wing or neo-fascist gangs then roaming the streets, their moment imminent, was responsible. A custodian, a mail clerk, and a young editorial assistant had died of smoke inhalation. Quite the offensive on the intelligentsia. The other victims, however, were the novels in the print shop, still in the midst of being bound, and this included Calque's newest, a fictionalization of her love affairs, all the participants perfectly recognizable, though portrayed in grotesque and radiant distortion. This trueness to life, as well as the novel's radical sexual politics, would no doubt have won it considerable if not positive attention. But only six weeks after the fire came the coup, and nationwide there was little attention left for literature. By the time anyone could have tried to salvage the lost novels, the military regime was in its furious first round of censorship and reforms, and Calque had withdrawn in illness to her apartment, in the first stages of the malaise that would find her years later immensely and debilitatingly fat.

I do not deceive myself. I know the novel is flawed, knew it the first time I read it, at my desk turning the pages with care and sitting quite upright. Calque's work is so sickeningly violent, and yet I succumb, each time it offers up a sentimental morsel, too sweet, I know, but swallow anyway, and in the throat it is monstrous, a moth with razor-edged wings. It is never wise to read her fiction quite alone, as I did then, around me the building a series of settling and humming sounds, growing louder as the novel's lovers destroyed one another, with grisly intimacy, as if the tongue could lift skin clean off bone. Perhaps it was in this vulnerable state—sitting in my office, teaching too much in those days and still alone in the city, my fingers crept to the lap of my skirt as I read, Calque's lovers encountering one another in cinemas (of course), in baths, and by the light of an aquarium—that I fell in love with the novel. Despite its flaws. Despite or because of. As they say. But I have reread it, at least a dozen times.

I wrote the introduction to the translation, which came out a few years later, and my paper on Calque's oeuvre, which focused on this novel as stylistic keystone, the last as it was to be written before her psychiatric treatments commenced, had been lauded, contended with, and was if not essential certainly a significant contribution to my vita when I was named chair. Calque is not of course the primary focus of my research; rather the poetry of that time, in the publishing wasteland left in the wake of the coup, no one able or desiring to publish under the censorship of the military regime, and so appearing in journals and underground publications across the continent, engaging in a bewitchingly fertile series of translations and collaborations with foreign artists in an effort to resist the cultural ruination taking place in their homeland. With her French name and French father Calque could have fled for Paris, but she did not. By that time she was too ill. And, she claimed, she hated Paris.

She claimed, in fact, that she hated everywhere that was not her apartment. *Where I was a girl*, she said in interviews, *hiding in the cupboards with my cousin during dinner parties, listening to every small thing that went on.* Consider how debauched her mother's parties were, how notorious. Shortly after he reached puberty the cousin became quite volatile, his psychiatric problems ultimately not unlike Calque's, but he was a boy, and big, and when he broke the arm of a teacher in one of his spells, he was sent to his first institution, and died some fifty years later in his fourth. And so Calque spent the coup years in her apartment, writing little, and occasionally, when illness overtook her, traveling to a northern hospital to convalesce, a luxury not widely available under the new regime, but with her mother's money she could seek out what vestiges remained.

Calque did not travel well, as I had explained in my papers, and my central illustration of this fact and of her instability in those days was the story of the photographer. She had stayed with the photographer in America only a few months, and yet what a wreck she'd been on returning, her symptoms heightening so that she would never again go abroad; and this could fairly be said to be the only time in her forty-nine years that she turned to drink.

My most thorough treatment of the photographer was in the chapter on Calque in my book on the art of the coup years, a chapter developed and adapted from my many previous critical writings on her life and work. By my reading, the writer's disastrous relationship with the photographer paralleled, if not signified, the relationship between their two nations. She: under siege, desperate, world-renowned art on the verge of exile, in a fight for its very existence. He: in the nascence of his talents, wealthy, hardly knowing his own power, recent tribulations overcome and his success merely in its first flowering. Anastasia had seen some of his work and after an ardent correspondence had traveled to New York to see him. Her first novel had met with some success, despite its controversial subject and the increasingly grim state of her country; she was high with her new status, if not manic. She packed up and flew to him.

Each marriage is the story of a marriage, and who is dead in the end.

And now, after years of dormancy, the story resumes: last week the photographer wrote to me. My book has been out almost a decade, but here was my chapter on Calque, Xeroxed and mailed back to me, with his enraged cover letter and that line crudely emphasized. I am not dead, the photographer wrote, you may be quite dismayed to learn. And all you have written about me are lies.

He must be in his early eighties now, but he was quite articulate and his penmanship picturesque. The English translation of the novel in which he appeared, the same *Eyes of the Moth*, had come out twelve years ago, several years before my own book. Yet it seemed that all this had escaped his notice until now, when it left him belatedly apoplectic—dangerously so, I thought, considering his age, and impressed that even as his insults mounted his handwriting did not waver. It was interesting that more of her lovers had not protested her treatment of them, whether in life or literature; the E who had sought out her manuscripts was the only one as far as I knew whom she had not pinned down cruelly in a novel somewhere, though I've wondered if this kindness was strategic, since E's new husband had proved himself such an adept translator.

Pure libel, the photographer wrote, and demanded immediate redress. His first example was that I had explained—as Calque said many times through the years—that on her arrival in New York he had refused to take her picture because she was too fat. This, she said in interviews, in her murmuring voice and with her cat-like expression, this broke my heart. He would only photograph my ankles, she said, which are still very beautiful.

Soon, she said, he only photographed women with ankles like mine. If you look closely, she said, you'll see the likeness, all the ankles are mine.

Utter nonsense, the photographer wrote. Though I, who had pored over what slides of his work I could find (he had not, in fact, become the success his early shows had promised; after the reviews cooled then ceased altogether, he had turned to advertising and worked now for a mid-range watch company, among others), believed I could see just what she meant.

Dear sir, I began in reply. Thank you for your letter. The novel has two sides; I would say it is two mirrors back to back. Any I is split from the start: two faces made one, the stone and the acid that bleeds it. I have forgotten your work, but I do remember Calque's ankles, perfect half-moons, expensive shoes resting on the platforms of her wheelchair. We shook hands.

In the novel the photographer is less than a beast: one-dimensional. Every day the woman flees him; he closes the door to his studio and she takes a train into the city, where she seeks out a neighborhood known for its radicals as well as its junkies. All day she sits in a dark room and hears a chorus of laughter and vomit and copulation, a woman tirelessly serenading herself. An old man befriends her, amateur gnostic, long-time addict. With him she pretends to pray. Though insincerely, merely to quiet his fears for her.

The photographer is passionate about Eastern thought and eats one meal a day, always in some sort of broth. She hides all her chocolate, which he is sick even to look at. The day she leaves him there is an ice storm, ice sheathing every twig of the oaks on the boulevard that leads to his house, ice on the tracks shutting down the trains that run from the suburbs into the city, ice snapping whole branches to litter roads and smash porches and roofs. She is caught in a police sweep of the building she passes her days in, but everyone else, it seems, had been warned; she is the only one there. After her release she flies home. Her clothes are stained with chocolate and she has grown only fatter.

Why must I write what you've already read? When he loses her the photographer believes he has known suffering, but he is mistaken. I do not know whether years later he marries.

Calque was nowhere near radical enough for her fellow intellectuals under the right-wing regime. In time they condemned her, expelled her from their journals, their collaborations, their salons. She wrote only of sex and children and God. When I met her she asked me, You didn't bring your daughter? I said, No. I said, I hadn't realized I'd told you about her. (Louisa was so young then, just two, and the research trip on which I met Calque my first time away from her.) Of course I could tell from your voice, Anastasia said, on the phone you have the voice of a mother. She laughed, and her nurse, with whom she had no languages in common, laughed with her.

Calque never had children and by then her husband was dead.

Years later she drowned, a seemingly accidental result of her medications and an oversized bathtub.

I wrote my letter to the photographer in the margins of the novel, on only the pages in which he appears. Not the translation, but the original: one of the rare few extant copies, which I had through years of diligence at last acquired. It was a gift, then, of some value, or would have been had I not defaced it. He had never learned her language, of course. Calque was—all agreed—a linguistic genius, and learned English as though it were an extended joke, punchline delayed; she claimed she learned only from television programs, but her vocabulary was multifarious and syntax dizzying. To this I myself can attest. She knew when she wrote the story of the photographer that he couldn't read it; it was only upon the translation of *Eyes of the Moth*, after her death, and with my own writing about her that he could learn the role she'd assigned him. He told me Anastasia had read him everything she'd written, in her own flawless translations, as they sat on the porch among the fireflies and lush green of Westchester County. I did not believe him.

From the novel Strawberry Fields, *selected for the Fence Modern Prize in Prose and forthcoming from Fence Books in 2018.*

As If Raising A Flag For An Unknown Country That Is One's Own

There is an old woman on the roof of her house waving a flag. The flag is not really a flag but a piece of linen with knots and stains. The woman on the roof waving the flag sings a song. You may have heard this song; it is a lullaby. Inside of her house the radio is playing, and the dogs are pulling cushions apart. There are stacks of boxes and newspapers all across the house. And books. The old woman is wearing a long nightgown that fills with wind. And the wind is a gust that comes from below. Meanwhile, a bird is being torn apart on the kitchen table by the dying cat and the feral one. The backdoor has slammed shut, and it is at least one hundred and four degrees in the shade.

The woman on the roof is waving the flag and singing into the gusts of wind. She has her gray hair tied into a knot. The woman is not at all crazy. But she had an uncle die from spinal meningitis and another, who built a rubber emporium in Brazil, die of malaria in his hut. Every single surface in the house is taken up by piles of papers, candles in wrapping paper. This is the South. At night it smells of fire and ash. The place is experiencing a drought. It is no longer a desert. It is a drought. But right now the sun is sinking, and the bird is torn to shreds. The woman on the roof has never suffered hunger, nor does she own a pistol. She has seen every road in Mexico and some in Guatemala and Nicaragua. There are blue veins like rivers along her legs.

She used to be a pipe smoker. Inside of the house most of the dogs are barking. Inside of the house it is hotter than on the roof from which you can see the expanse of the town.

Once she and her family traded an old car for a hundred and twelve raincoats, which they sold by the coast to buy the fare back to the States on a banana freighter. They took the coati with them. The coati ate a large hole into their apartment wall. Inside of the house is an album filled with yellowed newspaper articles on homicides. The articles are in Spanish. The album is a former executive binder for Christmas cards. The linen flag is waving. You might ask, why stand on a roof with a linen flag? Why be called names? Why risk Nicaragua and dictators? The uncle in Brazil was found after a few days by a housekeeper or servant. Brazilian bats from

Mexico migrate to North America in the summer and settle in abandoned iron ore caves. At dusk—soundless—they lift as one, out of the bombed rock. The woman is a widow and has not seen snow in years. In the living room there is a crazy quilt, which is framed, and a book on Brando and little beds for the dogs, canned food. She is on the roof, the old woman. She is, and one does not know why or if she will ever come down again. The cats meanwhile have multiplied. Unlike the baboons in Sumatra, who commit infanticide, the cats lick their babies. The house has various courtyards with tables and chairs covered in birdshit, which is covered in ants.

A lizard moves vertically across the wall. Ice cubes brush the glass and separate in a humble clonk.

The banana freighter got caught in a typhoon back then, and she lay sick in the captain's cabin. Every six hours the captain would bring her turtle soup. And the boat drove vertically up against the waves before crashing back down until they reached the coast of Florida. There the boatmen from Honduras avoided the streets and sent her out to collect the mail and money. They weren't used to this kind of treatment.

The woman looks older than her age. She just does, and her back hurts her. She was in a car wreck when pregnant with her first child. With all the dogs in the back of the pickup and her husband, who landed his legs in a cactus. Afterwards, she chased the dogs for a long time through the fields. The sun is a small red ball in the distance, caught between two craggy mountaintops. The crazy quilt came all the way from Washington D.C., the articles on homicides from Mexico and Nicaragua, where her grandfather once worked in the mahogany business. Mahogany is a very expensive wood. During her third trip through Mexico, her money was stolen. The money that had to last for the next six months. She saw the men who broke into the car. It was a small village. Every day she spread the news in the pharmacy, at the market, in the liquor store about the men who had stolen her money. The village knew who the men were. Eventually, she was presented with all her belongings laid out on a table ceremoniously, an elderly woman blessing each item.

When the sun has finally dropped behind the mountains and into someone else's morning, this story will end. Even if the woman continues to hold the linen flag on her roof. Even if she decides to come back down or, god forbid, to fling herself from the roof. She seems to have none of these intentions. She seems unaware of this story happening at all.

In Kleberg County on the South Texan coast, a woman had been living on the beach with her two children for the past eight months before moving into a trailer park close to a border town. She was interviewed by the Sheriff's deputy last September. The woman told the Sheriff that she and her children were staying on the beach as a learning experience while on vacation from New York. She said she took baths in the bay and occasionally at the gas station. She showed him some cash, out-of-state food stamps, and a pistol that she kept for protection while they traveled. The story was told on the radio after the standoff and shooting. You might ask, why tell stories to tell other stories? Why not clean the house? Why leave the doors in the house unlocked? The baboons in Kenya do not commit infanticide. From the roof you can see the road to Mexico, although the old woman does not cross the border any longer. She does not desire the breath of Guadalajara anymore. Some rattlesnakes out there too.

The coati grew very tame and loving, nuzzling everyone's ears. But eventually the apartment had too many holes. They traveled and slept outside on tarps, below trees. The woman cannot swim, which she felt to be an advantage on the banana freighter because she would die first, suffering shorter. There might have been a moment in the captain's cabin when the captain became a little too worried, a little too caring about her seasickness. But the woman was even then, as a young girl, fearless. You might ask, why go to the hardest places? Why be poor? Why eat whatever there is? The old woman on the roof rolls her eyes, maybe smiles.

Road kill was always carried to the other side of the road. The peaches in the basket are from the trees in the neighborhood. It is pecan season. It is chili season. It is hot season. It is a year filled with memories and unfinished projects. At a café across town, a friend of the old woman is telling her students about cruelty. Or is the word that she uses "evil?" She is drinking coffee and eating sweet bread. This woman also has ties to Mexico, where she saw Diego Rivera once give a lecture in the dark holding a candle below his chin. "Let's be honest, he was ugly," she says.

The old woman has decided to sit down on the tiles of her roof. She has taken the linen off the pole and wrapped it around her body. As already mentioned, the sun is sinking.

The cats have entirely disposed of the bird torn to shreds, not even a feather on the table. You might ask, why let your skin be dried up in the sun? Why have a failing cooling system? Why not go north? Back then a family passport was sufficient for travel. Her mother read every single book in the school library. Her father was born to sharecroppers. The bird shrieked "east," and then flew south.

A day earlier, during a dinner party, someone posed a hypothetical poll question to a group of eight. If the earth had ten more years to live, would you stay or take a shuttle to a newly discovered mud planet? A man suggested eroding moon craters rather than the Amazon. And out of eight, six voted to leave the earth to shuttle to the mud planet, and two voted to stay and see the last decade of prodigy and swan shit.

The old woman has a stomach of steel. But you might ask, why make the trip when you know you will get sick? They took the banana freighter many more times but stopped eating bananas. The sun has now officially moved on. The colors are dimming, except the linen flag around her body, which shines on into the evening. She can trace her bloodline back to a Native American great-grandfather who, at one point, held a hundred slaves. But she looks rather Rumanian. There is a grey, gauzy film across her eyes. The back problems may be a direct consequence of the many thousands of miles she rode in the backseats of old cars across the continent.

There is a story of her car that broke down in Mexico, in the middle of nowhere. It was fixed by passengers of a local bus passing in the afternoon heat. You might add that life is not a wish list. Some women on the bus made coffee and shared their pastries. In the house there is a painting of women washing in the river. There is a fine layer of dust on each item in the house. The dogs begin to get nervous; they jump up to see out of the windows. They call her name. They bark and howl. The walls are rattling. The ants stream out of the walls. She laughs on the roof. How did she get herself up there? The sun is reddest before it goes, an all-powerful expression that settles on cacti and sand, on cows' backs in the valley, the lights. She has children down there. She can ingest most things, even mold, transformed milk, the wilder dirt of the dogs' saliva in her water. And their snouts are all flat on the floor, as if praying. The dogs will bark until hoarse. She is holding her stomach; there is finally some pain. She was an only child, and when she was born the doctor said, "Oh my, another girl." Her mother read *Walden* to her in the hospital. You might ask, why be a daughter? Why sense the need? Time has been all over the house, and each clock shows a different constellation. In the living room it is always afternoon. Everything falls asleep in the afternoon. The heat depletes the blood, the air thick as blood. Everything nods off and falls from its position. The sleeping house becomes distracted from its own aging existence. And nothing indicates any end. You might ask, why end?

This story appears as "Flag" in Uncountry: A Mythology.

TOM HAVIV

Didactic Poem

FLAG INVENTION I

In 1909, in Istanbul, a student-run organization devel-
loped the Pan-Arab flag, its colors lifted from a   13th
century poem by Safi al-Din Al-Hilli   (when   *sublime
feelings his heart fill*). In 1914, Paris, the Young Arab
Society designed a new iteration of the flag (Hussein
Sharif added the color red),   which was adopted in
                                1916 (Arab Revolt)
                                1948 (Naqba).
consider —*sing*— the dates:

        1909, 1914, 1916, 1948, 1967, 2015

FLAG INVENTION II

In 1885, in Rishon LeZion, Fanny Abramovitch   and
Israel Belkind designed the "Flag of Judah" (*bring
witness the swords, did we lose hope*)   as a marker
of a new settlement. In 1897,   Switzerland,
Morris Harris, a New Yorker,   presented a design
for the flag of a new state, which was adopted in
                        1898 (Second Zionist Congress)
                        1948 (War of Independence).

consider —*sing*— the dates:
          1885, 1897, 1898, 1948, 1967, 2015

NATIONAL SONG

During the final note of national song, which is the
longest, begin to disassemble the machinery of cit-
izenship. Or if the song is just beginning, but is held
in fermata, begin screaming. the *gestureless salute*
may be used: no arms raised, never facing the flag,
only your neighbor, mouth closed. As soon as pa-
triotic effect is desired, incinerate the flag. Use its
ash to paint lines of flight. Foxtails are burning. The
buildings are swept aside like wheat. *Salute*: repeat.

OCEAN

Beneath the ocean, the divine body, the deflection of a sequence of forms, marching into the unending   ordering of. One pole projecting into sky.   Another deeper into ocean. The ocean of obstructions.   The charge on the individual. The charge on many: on those bodies who bend the perimeter of other bodies. Watch the flag through optical obstructions (your bedroom window, school window, stained glass,   LCD [ion-strengthened   glass, antinomy, boron], ice.)

BENT FLAG POLE

In a domain   in which a wall of light diffuses our attention, there is a flag pole. The flag pole has the flag of a nation on it. It is not necessarily a nation that you recognize [the necessary action]. Pick up the flag briskly lower it, raise it,   ceremoniously lower it, remove it. Rush into the wall of light. Tomorrow, you may begin by breathing.   You   may   begin by wondering   what kind of projection this pole is, what kind of wall may be passed through,   perceived.

OTHER FLAGS

Before the aftermath, during hours of darkness,   the
flag must be fully illuminated.   Remain silent; it will
be seen. Ordinarily, the flag should be displayed in the
sun. Cyclones, war, siege, electrical fire may remove it.
No superior prominence than when it seeks no honor.
Other flags raised nearby must stand. The palm, syntagm.
In a time of peace; in a time of internationalism.
The flag: the bright bits of flame   in a long sequence of bodies, the durational hum of passing eras.

OF

Of it, if, from about behind the of now for for the under through. Into, off belonged to, to the flag. Over o-ver over, the within of into first The widened-from, the fear of into Domain, child, out of, out of leisure, across love; when the exquisite becomes expedient the revolution has begun.

Begin each action with a preposition: "where to," she says. Home or out. From home, back home, or into the world?

THE

These are the strong words that carry more weight than words, this is the game that we established when we were young. The ocean was the great skin. The ocean laughed while we were asking. The body, the earth, the white night, never woken to. We called our nation: birth.

Behind each preposition: the situation at hand. Our hand towards, for, the mouth of a larger morning:
night, unclosed

Part II of "A Flag of No Nation" *sequence.*

URAYOÁN NOEL

en flor ida

Feeling kind of well worn   in Melbourne   ringing my summer bell
horn   making my summer noises   the winter   quiets me again   and
my words   start to splinter   into that   shared nothingness   bound by
snow   and interrupted speech acts   I'm brandishing my digital pick-axe
and hashtagging my pics at   another pixelated world   why are folks so
elated   by pics anyway?   biopics   picky about their movies   picking at
their plates   as if it just   weren't more food to be thrown away   más
comida para ser botada   más despedidas   más huidas   más pasadías por
carreteras   I'm walking on the side of the road   fully aware   there is no
road   there are only sides   besides   nothing is recordable   all records
are full of b-sides   even in the age of mp3s   I can be the lady   with the
beehive hairdo   singing a blues   to the who's who   of the exurban
ricanstruction crew   that's right   I said Rican   eso fue lo que dije   I
know where I am   en la Florida   somewhere   down the middle   it
ain't no riddle   aquí se hace vida   la diáspora se construye su avenida
nombremos el abandono de la isla   aquí donde la brisa   no aterriza   más
bien se   digitaliza   el Melbourne that I knew   estaba in Australia
down under   down south   but I guess everywhere   Boricuas are   is
the global south   the American south   sureños huraños   I guess
Melbourne   is where I'm reborn next   no Melbourne conspiracy   nor
ultimatum   últimamente   como que duele esto de improvisar   lo
imprevisible de rimar   otra epopeya   al frente de Popeyes   papá ya tú
sabes   lo que se dice y se desdice   lo que se hace y se deshace   aquí en
Buena Vida Estates   estate quieto   estate ready   pa la buena vida   te lo
digo yo   la buena diva   qué es eso de continuing care?   qué es eso de
retirement?   qué es eso de community?   si ya nadie se retira   si no hay
plan de retiro   si todos estamos sin plan   derretidos   en un trópico
imposible   y qué es eso   de un negocio que se llama Cheddar?   qué es
eso?   queso!   el queso que tengo está bien fuerte!   diablo qué vulgaridad!
I guess that's what happens when you improvise   down inexistent streets
somewhere   en la Florida   todavía no redimida   poetas de mi vida   quién
de ustedes adivina?   los que vivimos in this vicinity   todos underground
todos cargando telephones   smart or not   todos con cable o sin cable

pero siempre en peligro   under warnings   global warming también   eso
sí que se siente   el escalofrío de estar vivo   por estas coordenadas   pero
que no suene a llantén   a llanta sin repuesta   todo tiene su final   todo tiene
su respuesta   aunque sobren las preguntas   porque en verdad   hablo
desde el privilegio   el privilegio de los que estamos acá   el privilegio del
poeta con su   jajaja   poeta político   poeta social   el privilegio del verbo
como un Amado Nervo   más acerbo y feisbuquiante   el privilegio del
sortilegio cuasi-compartible   después de todo eso es ser poeta   la desdicha
de mis speech acts   export sodas con salchicha   taking selfies at the
beach   supongo que con eso basta   ya con eso somos boris   recordando
UB40   I be almost forty   con o sin 40s   pa bajarme en la playa   pa
bajarnos las tangas mentales   a fuerza de fritolanga   y besuquearnos en los
matorrales   neuronales   te conté la de la alabanza a la torre de Cialis   está
fuerte   está duro   Cialis as in   se alisa el pelo   nos creemos blancos
nos creemos inmunes a la bancarrota   nos creemos performeros   de la
derrota utópica   pasando por otro Pier 1 Import   haciendo piruetas   sin
que a nadie le importe   todo en Puerto Rico es importado   salvo lo que es
exportado   a lugares como Florida   entre ellos este servidor   en la flor de la
ida   y de la huida   whatcha gonna do about that?   yo soy el character
generator del verso   creando CGIs   en el TGI sin Fridays   en la semana
que nunca acaba   el hombre que no trabajó lunes   sino que perdió su
trabajo   y lo recuperó en forma de improvisaciones   telefónicas   toda labor
ahora es casualizada   part-time   sin beneficios   te lo digo yo   o mi
nombre es Bonifacio   tal vez haya chiripas en New Image Dentistry   pa
ser recepcionista   y devolverle la sonrisa   a una isla sin riposta   esto de
los cruces   nunca lo he entendido   porque soy de una isla   y en la isla no
conocen fronteras   salvo las linderas   de las laderas interiores   me están
mirando raro   persona non grata   o persona que grita   en la Florida   a flor
de piel   archipiélago en flor   floripondio floripondiando   el Flor Meléndez
del deporte verbal   no te equivoques   don't get confused   farm stores
express   as in express yourself   seamos el farm system de la palabra
posible   de la palabra drive-thru   sirviendo carros   desde 1957   cuando
nos modernizamos   del campo al pueblo   salimos de la ruralía   botaron de
la isla   a los pobres   a los negros   a los freaks   a los nacionalistas   a las
mujeres que no se dejaban domar   botaron a toelmundo   y nos creamos
nuestras propias   capitales decoloniales   lejos de las sucursales de
cafetales   y escribimos nuestros libros   libros que no se consiguen en
Barnes and Noble   libros megafónicos   por lo poco Amazónicos   historias
sin escribir   historia que hay que improvisar   "pa eso están los smartphones

pana"   "that's why we're digital these days"   "new kinds of connectivity"
"hashtag community"   o   sencillamente basta ya de hashtags   y basta ya
de com   y pensemos en la unidad irreducible del ritmo   ritmo corazonudo
ritmo propio   ritmo impropio   que no cabe   por estas 65s interminables
ritmos variables   volubles   que son el adoquín   que no cabe en Burger
King   el chinche sin mattress   sin firma pero firme   we're in the south
y'all   nearing a Lens Crafters   because really what we do as artists   as
beings of a digital netherworld   is craft our own lenseses   lenseses?
our own porous optics   our own ways of relating and becoming   our
own believable selves   storefronts of the sign   sabes el camino   con o
sin mattress   con o sin catre?   estamos perdidos?   diatre!   todo es strip
mall   stripped of meaning   nunca he ido a Hong Kong   hace tiempo que
no como popcorn   ni concón con tostón   pero vivimos en el super buffet
del cafetal neoliberal   a fuerza de puya   cada uno se hace su trulla   y te
canto mi booyah!   as in la bulla que busco   improvisando Lambrusco lírico
a lo brusco   no soy poeta de Cuzco   pero soy colonial   dándole casco a mi
asco   me rasco la roncha   donde renazco   ponchando   de cuando en
cuando con mi gente   metiéndole el diente   sediento   a la promesa de mi
musa   pero no hay biker que valga   pa improvisar ahora   soy loco pero sin
motora   get your motor running!   mi baika es prosaica   Lambrusco sin
Prosecco   no hay nada más pro   que el eco telefónico   en un país que
promete castillas   pero te deja en villas   don't wanna be ya   te vende
vitaminas   pero te extermina   y contamina la mina del espíritu   eso quedó
medio cursi   and I don't mean Gregory Corso   esto del Steak and Shake
was a mistake   but when you improvise   there's no mistake   because
there's no remake   or rather   meaning is always made and remade   no
reminder   to find your voice   and who knows   maybe some breeze
maybe the debris of meaning   maybe the awning   of the dawn of the
spondee   I'm putting the cheap in Chipotle   y sé que lo barato sale caro
pero sale   y sigue saliendo   y a lo que apuesto   es a ese seguir saliendo
aunque sin sobresalir   there's something about speaking   in a parking lot
you speak a lot   everything is allotted   and nothing is allowed   all the
more reason   to claim this parking lot   as if it were the street   as my
own mental barrio   as a space   for the post-millennial flâneur   except
this flâneur   isn't so much into flan   just call me ur   ayoán   what's
wrong with flan?   too sweet?   although really   no more sickly sweet
than what I'm doing here   giving you the democratic? words   with a
political? veneer   and claiming my smartphone   as extension of the
street   yeah like that's gonna work   as if we weren't in Tire Kingdom

as if these kingdoms hadn't made us all tired   retiring us from ourselves
devolviéndonos a los bus stops   al space coast   así es   estamos en las
costas espaciales   de ripostas irreales   estamos apostando a un futuro
que llega o no llega   como la guagua en la parada   donde se pudre el yo
gomas a la venta   y el llanto de las llantas   y el quebranto de mi canto   y
las revoluciones científicas de estas cunetas   gracias Thomas Kuhn   por el
etos   por dejarnos leerlas   con ti mascamos   nos remecemos en la cuna
renacemos en lugares   como Melbourne   el son de la loma es sus gomas
el conducir   sin conducción   que es nuestra única especie   de improvisar
de allanar   el bulevar interior   y de deshojar   la ciudad en flor

West Melbourne FL, 2015

LUCY BURNS

Almost Gone

Here in heaven
everybody had
just like that

lived in myth I
had illustrated
my life had

stayed on stayed years
in the neighborhood
walked as War-

hol walked before
Kansas City nights
before Eve

lived with me New
York actually a couple

of me showed up
and stayed true just stayed
strolling I

was residing
writing simply was
anywhere

in cut off jeans
on a train between
war candy

was so cool so
drunk gas pump drunk
almost a

heron landing
almost on
the sidewalk

MARI CHRISTMAS

Woodland

SMALL ACTS

I got my period the summer I was twelve. I didn't tell anyone. Mom had her hands full, and Willy was slipping through the cracks. Our mother worked at a hardware store downtown that mostly sold packing supplies and the occasional small tool. Their most popular items were replacement handles for brooms and mops. Kids from our neighborhood used these to smash mailboxes in the nicer suburbs. I once read somewhere that Mother Teresa prayed for small deeds to be done out of great love. So, in a sense, the store offered a counter service: administering small acts with intense hatred. These guaranteed the same results, and things around here tended to be peaceful.

While I was at the hardware store, Grandma Geraldine watched Willy. Willy was four and going through a phase where he thought he was a dog, and insisted on being tied to the clothesline. When Geraldine found him crapping in the chrysanthemums, she became the only one who took Willy seriously. She had her eyes trained on him, squinting and suspecting that any second he'd steal her food or run off with one of her foam hair curlers in his mouth. Sometimes Willy would jump onto the couch and she would baste his nose with the newspaper.

Uncle Mortimer and his boyfriend Floyd handed Geraldine off to us on the Fourth of July. The three of them were waiting on our front steps when we pulled up to the house. Uncle Mortimer had his arm slung around Floyd. It was hot as death inside our Camaro.

While Floyd unloaded Gearldine's suitcase from the truck bed, Uncle Mortimer led her down the porch and towards our car. Willy and I hung out the car window, gaping at Geraldine's hump, then at Mom, who began whacking her brother with her handbag.

Floyd whistled.

Then they drove away, hollering at Geraldine not to blow it. I pushed Willy out of the car. Geraldine stood there like it was the dawn of her execution and saw this as an occasion to lie down. Willy began furiously sniffing the suitcase, then comforted Geraldine by licking her hands, and she let him, playing dead. The shock of abandonment had momentarily paralyzed her.

Mom left Geraldine splayed out and dirt-covered, and began unpacking the sodas from the backseat. Then she used her foot to nudge Geraldine like something she had hit with the Camaro. Meanwhile Willy entertained himself by slapping Geraldine's bare ankles, which were already turning pink from the sun.

"You're killing me!" Geraldine suddenly shouted, springing to life. Willy let out a yip.

"For God's sake, die upstairs and not in front of the children. You look like an omen," said Mom. When Geraldine refused to move, we tried rolling her to the porch.

"I am too heavy to die up there!" Geraldine screamed from the ground. "When I die," she said giving us the finger, "you'll have to ride my body down the stairs like a sled!"

Somehow Mom managed to talk her into the house. Once inside, Geraldine began unloading her jewelry and announcing who was getting what.

"You, Sissy," she said, stabbing me in the arm with the broach, "get nothing." Mom turned herself into a living, breathing barrier, but by then I was sure I had tetanus.

"Let this be a lesson, Cecelia Anne," she said as dots of blood appeared along my arm. For the next few days Geraldine dragged herself around the house. A wounded animal, her sunburnt lips clamped around a bottle of Night Train like a bear trap.

DISTANCE

In the mornings, I would go to the hardware store and wipe down the counters and set up the displays while Mom answered the phone and dropped rolls of quarters into the registers. Then I'd lock the doors and do whippets in the back room. It was messy. Cans of dried paint lined the walls. I liked to sit there and feel the room wrap itself around me and begin to feel familiar again. Then I would take another hit.

The two women who worked the front were very religious. They didn't know anything about paint. The store would have gone out of business if it weren't for all the nostalgia. They used to get letters. Some were encouraging, and these they stapled to the front bulletin. One couple sent a note with a newspaper clipping of their wedding announcement and a check. Underneath it they wrote: "I know you'll always be there wishing us all the happiness possible in our life together—even when we fall apart." Taped to it was a picture of a porch, their latest DIY project. It was a nice letter.

Mom's two coworkers were devout. They had pushed the desks together, creating a long table like the one from the Last Supper. The older of the two was always dropping boxes of pens. She would find me in the back room lying on the table, feeling dicked all up and down. She had the habit of coming in and tearing long strips of cardboard while reciting passages from the New Testament. She would do that for me. Afterwards she'd sweep the pieces into a pile in the corner. She was an anxious woman but at least she was very neat and apologetic about it.

The other woman carved cross insignias and pictures of small animals into soap. She had an online business and over her breaks would show me photos documenting her creative process. One was of her and the lazy prostitutes of the Quickie Mart. Another showed blocks of Dial and Ivory being unwrapped over the trashcan in her apartment. Her favorite carving oscillated between a dove and a squirrel, but if she asked me what I thought I always responded, "the dove." If I was high, I pulled my shirt up and over my throat.

This one had a daughter who was trying to make it big in L.A. and would receive boxes filled with headshots and scraps of paper asking for money. She would bring these into work, arranging the photographs above the table in the backroom and weeping at the altar she had created while I spastically lost consciousness, amped out of my mind.

"If you only brushed your hair," she said once, holding up a headshot and closing one eye, "you'd be sisters." Then she attempted to stroke my face from across the room.

SNOW

The winter before Geraldine arrived was the kind that grabbed at you. The sun was unbelievably cold and white. On Sundays Mom huddled under blankets and swilled brandy before falling back asleep. I took Willy on walks when the sidewalks weren't horrid. In the evenings I played cribbage online with a retiree named El Dude.

Mom's nerves were shot.

One evening my Uncle Floyd called.

"Give me a second to get out of the kitchen," Mom said, dragging the blankets behind her.

I could hardly hear her. The refrigerator was constantly shuddering and the heat banged when shut off. Every now and then snowplows grated by, throwing Willy into howls of desperation like a castaway spotting ships in the distance.

As she had Floyd repeat everything, I ran into the living room and picked up the second line. Geraldine was doing not-so-good. He and Mortimer were moving. At the end he wanted to know when they could drive down with her.

"I can pay you," he said. He gave Mom a figure.

"You can't take her with you?" she asked.

I stood there trying to get my thoughts going in one direction.

"I start in July. That'll give you enough time to put your things in order, right?"

All I knew of Geraldine was that, even when happy, she was the most horrible fall-down drunk. She would start with a pint of Bushmills and by noon she wouldn't be able to tell the difference between an amphitheater and an orgy. Her hump was some sort of liquor reservoir and her Depends were perennially springing leaks. She smelled sour, and if you sat next to her long enough you would start sweating and your head would begin to loll around.

The next morning Mom threw on her coat and clipped Willy to the kitchen table. The Camaro wouldn't start because of the cold so we walked to work. The streets were deserted and covered with a thin layer of white dust. It was very Los Alamos.

I knew that, by the time we arrived, the two coworkers would be outside, sweeping snow off the front walk. They were habitually antagonizing each other into being better Christians.

"Have you heard so-and-so is in the hospital again?" one would start.

"Oh my. I should call her."

"I think I'll stop by with a pie tonight. Her poor husband, Jesus, bless him." Stuff like that. Their parish was on the verge of an epidemic. Their God Tourettes made Mom edgy and she would make up excuses about needing to check the schedule in the office.

When we got to the hardware store, that's when she told me: Geraldine had cancer, the kind that suddenly appears on X-rays like a snow flurry. There was nothing we could do. We didn't have the money. Soon it would pile on, burying our house, the Camaro, the front yard, Willy and me et cetera, et cetera. She made it clear—there would be a specific silence following a hard snow like this: One where you can stand outside and hear the blood pumping through your chest. You are that alone.

After the whippets I slid off the table and put on my smock. I went outside. My eyes pinned on every leaf and petal while I sat in the greenhouse, waiting for the sprinklers to turn on. In the winter it was the closest thing to being alive. The world became a developing Polaroid and the knowledge of it all was somewhere above my head. I had a plan. If one of the coworkers found me, I'd sway my body to demonstrate spiritual ecstasy.

Mom applied for the job because she wanted to be someone who worked with flowers. I said I thought it could help. I liked the idea of watering and killing aphids and springtime. But there were timers and chemicals for this, and instead Mom worked the register hungover.

After I finished doing my Baby Moses in the Reeds routine, I worked the front. All afternoon I bagged the best I could. One of the women must have been pretending everyone was filing through for the Eucharist, because she waited for them to open their mouths before giving back their change. It was slow, but this had an effect. Sometimes she waited too long. A married man confessed his teenage girlfriend was having an abortion at the clinic down the street.

"I just had to tell somebody," he said afterward, embarrassed, and put his hand out.

I needed to get out of there.

I went into the back room, hung up my smock and stuffed one of the larger glossy headshots from the altar into my back pocket. Then, as if going underwater, I huffed some more acetone.

THE VIEW

I dragged Geraldine's suitcase into the old office we had cleaned out. She walked slowly around the room, never turning her back on me, and pointed to the sheets she wanted. They were yellow with small swirls of white flowers. Willy began to retch in the kitchen from eating too much crabgrass.

"My death bed should have a spectacular view of some mountains," she said as I tucked in the sheets. "Not some shithole where at 5 a.m. the grey light gets all over everything."

That night I found Geraldine in my room, sitting on the edge of the bed, jabbering to herself, and Willy gritching beside her.

Geraldine took up Willy's leash and snapped it like a rein.

"Look at me," she said, stamping her slippers. "I am cock-bald." Willy gazed at her, bewildered.

She carried photos of herself before the chemo.

"This is me," she whispered, showing us a picture of a woman with a permanent wearing a striped two-piece. It felt like a trick. I fixed her wig as she watched in the mirror. But I was the same; every morning I took the stolen glossy off my dresser and thought, "Look how much better you are today. Today is a new day."

The summer Geraldine moved in with us a strange pair of albino deer appeared in the woods behind our house. One morning, I found her sitting at the kitchen table making tinfoil animals.

"I've been seeing unicorns," she broadcasted, arranging her menagerie on a blanket of grey dryer lint and eyeing me suspiciously. If I hadn't seen the deer first, I would have assumed she was probably potted.

"The stags?" I asked. "You've seen them?"

She considered my question and I admired her handiwork. I couldn't imagine Geraldine looking out into the woods. Most mornings she buried herself under a pile of blankets, cursing Mortimer's life of hot sin and the deeds of sexually impotent Russians. I suppose she had seen the deer from the couch, the two stags, their whiteness boring holes through the trees.

"Is that what they are?" she said. "This, on top of last night's acid diarrhea, I thought I was being poisoned."

That afternoon she made a list of things covered by her insurance that we could do together. We took the bus to the clinic and had a couple of moles removed.

"Did you know," she said, placing a finger on each Band-Aid, "for your parents' last anniversary, they went back to the same spot where they first met just to see if they still liked each other?"

"Well?" I asked. "Did they?"

Geraldine gave me a look like I had never belonged to her.

But the next day she seemed to be in a celebratory kind of mood. She thanked the Lord for the bounty of breakfast she had received. She let Willy dart around with a pair of knee socks in his mouth. Around noon she announced she was tired of watching television and insisted I shove the couch over to the front window. Then we arranged the furniture so that the rooms continuously opened from one to another. When bored, Willy would trot around in circles like a show dog.

Afterward she poured me a drink.

"To men," she toasted. "There's one for every kind of morning."

That evening, over dinner, Geraldine brought up the albino deer. She dubbed them The Homos on account that they were both stags and were always seen traveling together.

"Like your uncles," she'd say.

She stopped falling asleep while trolling for smut on TV and began to stalk the deer from her window, pressing her fingers against pockets of scar tissue. Willy was allowed to join her, growling at things that weren't there, chewing on her Bible after she passed out.

EXTERMINATION

I stopped going to the hardware store that summer and found a job working for an exterminator where I was needed for a total of three hours: between four and six a.m and for an hour in the late afternoon when Geraldine and Willy were napping. By the time I'd come home Geraldine would be propped up in bed with Willy curled beside her like a croissant.

"I like this dog," she said after my first week. "You say a couple of nice things and it follows you around forever." Willy adored Geraldine. If she sat in the sun, he would have looked at her until he went blind. "This dog is my wife," Geraldine would say and give Willy a pat on the head.

The exterminator had a reputation for dealing with pigeons. In the afternoons we'd drive around setting out tiny dishes of poison and leaving them in various attics. The pigeons would never fly too far from the houses before they dropped. Then there they were, in front yards at dawn. I'd gather their stiff bodies while Paul sat in the hatchback, waiting for me to fill the bag. I'd work my way down the block, leading a chorus of barking dogs down the street, while Paul listened to the radio and told me, through the open window, to keep moving. We needed to be done before the families awoke. I had dark welts under my eyes and wandered from house to house like a newborn getting used to the light.

"A yard full of dead birds produces the sort of effect that is not part of the college plan," he would remind me. Some days Paul liked to imagine himself a duck hunter on a large Virginian estate. "Pull! Cecilia," he'd cry.

It was August now, and by afternoon it was too hot to stay inside. Geraldine wedged herself inside the refrigerator to stay cool. She would emerge ferally as if any second the metal latch would come down on a trap door. Willy dug holes in the yard and stayed cool by lying in them.

But the deer gave us something to do. After Paul dropped me off, I would wander around the woods collecting trash with Willy. I sought shade, pulled beer bottles from the creek, removed gum stuck to trees, while Geraldine scuttled around. The cancer drugs had made her mind loopier, her body weaker.

I thought about what I had found the other day by the creek, a plastic lunchbox full of used condoms that smelled like a bag of bad fast food and how I had gotten sick all over the bramble afterwards. I knew it was only a matter of time before something would happen to the deer. Our world was not safe. We expected everything. I would lie outside on the verge of heatstroke, high on Geraldine's ketamine and oxycodone, and have violent fantasies about coming across one of the deer lying on its side in a field or by the gas station, its white fur made whiter against the drying blood. Even Geraldine said the hand of God would sever The Homos' heads by the first frost. Then the news crew would arrive, maybe a couple of cops, and together we'd cut open the dead deer and find marbled, within its internal organs, syringes, severance checks, potato chip bags, diapers, pipe cleaners, and a couple of poisoned pigeons.

PERIOD

In the meantime Geraldine went about trying to acquire a rifle. Since she was too weak to leave the couch, she turned on us. She began first by complaining that she couldn't trust Willy and me to defend her.

"Against *what*?" asked Mom.

I reminded them both that Willy would do a fine job, considering he was practically rabid.

"You see? Even Sissy is afraid of the dog," Geraldine said, dragging me into it. Mom didn't correct her. Even she had given up calling Willy a child.

I put my hands up.

Geraldine said I had visions.

"I do not," I said.

Geraldine insisted. She accused me of maiming the truth. Then she went on about her infirm and vulnerable age. "I could be taken!" she argued. She reminded us that she was small and bald with limited movement.

"No one comes here," repeated Mom. "No one comes here to look at you."

"There was a man yesterday!" screamed Geraldine, becoming very Wagnerian. "A man! Tell her, Sissy!" she cried. "Tell your Mom how I couldn't protect myself. The things he wanted to do to me! Oh lord! His hands moved so fast."

Mom gave me the look.

"It was just an environmentalist," I said and shrugged.

"Hell would not have you!" Geraldine called out after Mom had left the living room. "Even if you were painted with the blood of Christ, Hell would not have you!"

I went outside. I had bled through my shorts that morning, and wrapped a wad of toilet paper around the crotch of my underwear. The birds were really playing their hits while I paraded my anxieties around the woods with the knowledge of a small massacre in my shorts.

I reminded myself that my birthday was coming up, and that when school started in a couple of weeks, I would be sprung from the jail that was my summer. Our school wasn't great but it had a sprinkler system. It was dependent on donations. The bushes in front were mangy shrubs full of white fungi that our teachers ashed their cigarettes into between classes. When our American flag tore during a storm, there was no money to replace it. The principal tried starting a collection but there were bigger issues—we had run out of toilet paper and the PTA office was overrun with patients from the methadone clinic. In another month I would be riding the bus. If I arrived early enough, I could trade Geraldine's meds with the addicts in the parking lot.

I loved riding the bus. Our family car was a dark red Camaro that sounded like a refrigerator being dragged down the street. When I got on the bus I couldn't take my eyes off the road. I imagined there were long green hills ahead of us, roads popping up and down like dolphins. There was a billboard of the ocean we always passed. It showed three teenagers out for a drive, and I liked to think they were yelling crude things at the surfers changing on the highway. I wanted to be sleeveless, to feel so happy as if I had a head injury or something. I wondered what it was like to walk on a beach, to hold a conch shell and collect sand dollars, that sort of thing. I had never been to the ocean. I wanted the wind to whip up sand and for a red bikini to floss my butt.

TROY

Mom told me this: That Geraldine was in the hospital. Underneath that hump she was bone-thin and her eyes swallowed everything. She could no longer keep her pills down. Her body barely withstood a strong wind. There was a war raging.

But not here.

The nurse assigned to her had a name tag that said Ruby, but Geraldine called her Helen. She was beautiful in an obvious, Nordic way, but gave the most watered-down smiles.

Sometimes we went into the maternity ward. The music was soothing in there. Geraldine scooted around incredulously, telling the pregnant women, "Did you know? They've figured out what causes that now."

Mom and Geraldine shared the same last name, and in the beginning, even Helen joked around, mistaking them for sisters.

"I'm the pretty one," Geraldine told Helen. "And the smart one. And the funny one."

With each round of chemo she would look much older, almost cadaverous.

"Would your grandmother like a newsletter?" a volunteer once asked as we stood in the lobby. Geraldine made a face. I took the newsletter and began wheeling us back.

"You are a cruel child," she muttered, reaching back and touching my hand like a compliment.

I sat outside Geraldine's room, vegging out on Mom's voice and imagining this tiny Trojan horse filled with crazed cells coursing through me. Helen was with her, sticking tiny swords into Geraldine's body. Mom's words were like breadcrumbs bringing me back. Next to the door, Geraldine's name was printed on a blue plaque and decorated with sparkly horse stickers. Willy was busy scraping them off.

FLIES

Mom got a second job at a local prep school twenty minutes from the hospital. She worked the mailroom. The school made me roll my eyes. I'd get off the bus and take Willy to its old gym where he would chase the substitute teachers running laps while I got drunk and crushed pills with other kids in the bathroom.

In this way, months passed.

There was a week of Athenian civic role-playing.

I dated a senior who didn't know how to kiss. He would hold my hand and rub his lips back and forth like he was grazing. It was a confusing time.

In the fall I gave handjobs like a rite of passage. I did this until the fun went out of it. By winter it was infuriating. With whatever was left of me at the end of the day, I visited Geraldine in the hospital with Mom and Willy.

I'd try to provoke her. I did things. I imitated the senior's kissing on her paper-thin skin. Then I sucked on my arms in a pattern that resembled a rash. When Helen came, I showed her. She gave me the most flat-footed look I had ever seen.

"Did you do that?" she asked. I noted no concern.

"It's very painful," I said. "Do you have something for it? It really itches."

"Shoo" Helen said.

"That's a lot of hickies," Geraldine said finally, and frowned.

"Is that what they are?" I asked.

LUNAR ECLIPSE

Two things. I got sober for the day and took Willy to the hospital. I regretted it immediately. It was like visiting a hole in the ground, like waking up in a bad ice age.

Geraldine had taped a sign to her door.

"I'VE HIDDEN EVERYONE'S MEDS AND CIGARETTES UNDER HERE WHERE NO ONE CAN FIT BUT ME. SO AS TO WHEN I'M COMING OUT, THE ANSWER IS NEVER."

"Mom?" Mom asked.

Geraldine poked her head out. She was eating the exact same sandwich that she had been eating since 4 p.m. yesterday. She was almost finished.

"You look really bad," she said to me, tugging on the cannulas up her nose.

It was true. Things felt clearer in a not-so-good way, and my vision kept rearranging the objects in her room.

"She just doesn't drink enough water," said Mom, her voice distant.

"I'm still not sure about this place," Geraldine was saying, "but I need to stretch."

"I could sneak you out," Mom offered.

"Nope, nope. I think you'd be very sneaky and that is good. I'm just not ready to start behaving like a ghost."

My knees throbbed so I sat by the window. Geraldine eventually came out. She was wearing a bathrobe. Willy had chewed off the string that kept it entirely closed. I saw and I didn't.

"I know what you're thinking," she said, leaning on my shoulder as Mom guided her from the chair to the bed. "Maybe if I drank and smoked and got cancer, I too could look this good."

Her lunacy was exhilarating. The truth was I should have been in a ward, but not this one.

That was almost a year ago. Tonight there is a lunar eclipse.

Mom helped her into fleece pajamas. Even though her mattress was covered in the kind of plastic that trapped heat and could easily be disinfected after discharge, Geraldine was cold all the time. I wanted to take her home, where we'd turn on the hot water and sit still in the steam like plants after dark.

The four of us went out to the field behind the hospital. When the wheelchair could go no farther, we carried her across the upturned earth like an animal sacrifice. I let go of Willy's leash and he scrambled ahead, whimpering in the dark. Then we sat with her in Mom's arms and waited for the moon to come out of hiding.

"This is what happens when there are no more natural predators," whispered Geraldine.

FIELD NOTES

I can't stand to think about how some people lead such beautiful lives while others' bones grow sick. From her room we watched a man fly his remote civilian drone in the field. Above, a hawk drifted in the sky.

I didn't have the thoughts you only have alone in the bathroom, you know. I had them everywhere. I had room for nothing else. I had stopped looking for the stags. I carried an extension cord in my backpack. I kept asking: "What about now?"

But I paid attention when the doctor lectured. Then I took a nap.

I dreamed Willy was outside, tethered to the clothesline. Geraldine was outside too, swearing loudly through her tin foil megaphone for Willy to find the scent, and watching me like you'd watch bad weather. It was summer again and the weight of her hump had her so bowed over she could barely undo the tether. Willy was pacing madly, practically drooling with excitement.

I followed her and Willy from the hospital and into the woods.

The sky was graying.

The geese bolted into the clouds.

I picked up a couple of beer cans to bring home while Geraldine rooted about the woods for alcohol like a truffle pig. Willy was barking at the egrets standing in the green water, and a couple of mallards swam against the current. I remembered the white deer and looked all around me. When I had first seen the stags that spring, two years ago, I thought they were giant lambs. They were so beautiful I about had an attack. It had been a while since I'd last seen them, and years before the white shapes began emerging on a doctor's scan, drawing Geraldine to us. I hoped the stags had gone from one safe place to another, stepping out of our world as they had entered it, as if by accident. I took my shoes off and walked into the river, troubling the water and feeling the snail shells crushing underfoot. I looked behind me. Geraldine had discovered a stash of half-empty Bud Lights and was swilling the last of it.

How do you orchestrate an ending?

I was riding down this road that was becoming exceedingly narrower. Even I knew there would eventually be no space to turn around.

I could tell you a lot about the truth, but then I'd have to write you a story.

In that story I wouldn't talk about Geraldine, or the sun, only how these things do not slip away.

When she died, I was in school. No one called to tell me. I took Willy to the hospital and found Floyd with his arms around Mortimer's hips. Mom sat in the hallway.

I felt ransacked.

I marched Willy to the animal shelter. He was quiet the whole way, walking with one arm between his legs like he used to, a scared dog.

Outside the door was a bleach dip for shoes.

When we got to the counter, a volunteer wearing a washed-out sweatshirt was filing papers and whistling. Then she saw us, and a look of impatience crossed her face.

I wanted to surprise myself.

"Which one goes down next?" I asked. It was freezing in there. I held my breath and followed her ponytail across the room and down the hallway to the kennels. They were like Stations of the Cross.

The volunteer got to the third kennel and stopped. She was pointing at a medium-sized black dog that looked right past us, but Willy reached in and rubbed at the yellow crust around its eyes. The dog shied away, and then came with its neck sticking out, wanting to lick his knuckle.

"Well, there goes your standing in the community," the volunteer said.

I filled out the forms, lied and said I was eighteen and could pay all my bills. I was so sad and tired, I looked it.

The dog was a girl, and in some ways it was a relief; we would not be returning with a hellhound or sex pest. I also found out she had a litter at the shelter. There were five of them. Her teats hung down like little party hats. I asked to borrow the phone. I called the hospital and listened to the automated reel before hanging up. We couldn't take the bus so the three of us walked. It was dark and the streetlights were lit up by the time we reached home.

I thought about Geraldine, years later, in the middle of a three-day coke binge with a pillow glued to my face and drool trickling down the corners of my mouth.

I remembered there was a guest book at the funeral and how I spoke their names.

I could almost feel the pressure of Willy's hand on my arm as I tied the dog to a post outside.

Hardly anyone showed, and no one we recognized. Everyone had given us up for dead a long time ago.

I picked up the pen.

"The dog is outside," I wrote. "Willy is beside me. There is a long line of people behind us waiting to say nice things about you. I am glad to be among them."

I lay wired to the night, always expecting something else.

"I'm not dead," the Geraldine in my brain would say, "still practicing. Sorry for the grim joke. Ha ha. But heads up: they put you inside a room where they leave you for a long, long time. Long enough for your body to make up its mind. Obviously I'm done with that now. Here I am."

KATHRYN MARIS

I have had a positional headache for two months

I've had a positional headache for two months &
a brain tumour is suspected so I will have an MRI.
I feel I have been killing myself, though the truth lies
in-between. As drinking is the one thing that
predictably exacerbates my headaches, I stopped.
Sometimes when I have binge-drunk, the pressure
at the top of my head is so great I have hallucinated,
like the time I thought Pascale had taken over my body.
These "glitch" moments are worrisome, like my certainty
there was a mirror in the kitchen (there never was) and
doors that were once on my right are now on my left.

What women want

After my best friend read a self-help book called *Make Your Own Fairy Tale* in which the author advises you to write your wish in a notebook and store it in the drawer of your bedside table, I did exactly that. One day my other half said, "For fuck's sake I don't understand what you want." When I suggested he look at the notebook in the bedside table, where my wish had been collecting dust for 3 years, he revealed he would never look at someone's private notebook, he was above that, and that was the end of the conversation.

AARON COLEMAN

Shadows Uplifted

A TRANSGRESSIVE TRANSLATION OF FRANCIS HARPER'S 1892 NOVEL *IOLA LEROY, OR, SHADOWS UPLIFTED*

I. ALL WAYS, THEY TAKE MY CHILDREN I contrive to tell you what I know you know. I wonder about what I can't tell you openly—and why. Make games, play lies accordingly. I am afraid. Everything about this world screams fear of fever. The old ones put their ears to the ground. They wait. They get a sense of what is coming and how to know when to go. I read what masters keep secret, speak to you of eggs and butter and blue clouds. Hear underneath speech and we will see what comes of this war, what will will come down like gravity, down to this South.

II. IN THE REBEL'S DIN I am not the only contraband. I may be a different region of the sky—may one day cover us. Those who see the blue or men beyond the woods run for one or both. These trees between worlds no longer hold the secrets where we used to meet. The old ones aren't all ready to let them go. Let the trees go. Let the secrets go. I can't let this skin go. I don't want to bloodlet home, go.

III. THE FATHER GENE In each movement, through the world, I taught myself a new I. I can love what is not yet and will become. Discarded I's fall slowly from my life like family. I stay put because I trust no home. I leave because I trust no home. Loving, I am believed to be—sick outside my body. Outside my mind. Sickness taught me love. Sickness taught this I to see—to see what dying slowly brings. I trust what remains in my eyes more. I am moon-white. I almost died. I was always almost dying.

IV. TOM FORGIVES My own release would never be enough. I'd die for a cause because I don't believe in dying. Blue better be better than gray, I tell you. I'm afraid to eat I'm so hungry. My throat's full of low country. I ain't hiding. Least not no more. This name Tom is barely mine. My name means no tomorrow. Can't you see me? See? Least let me see you over to who hides in the open.

V. NON-DREAM Don't you dare tell me a thing you think I don't know about me—about us. I know the doctor wants to plumb my fever. I know you're all feverish with fear of fire. I know. When I sing I hem fire. The hypocrite is eager. I refuse to kiss your fingers. Each day I forget again what was want. I'm wound and bandage. I'm known and unknown. Sold seven times in six weeks, they say. My skin whispers my blood's confessing. Your eyes—like my eyes used to, way back when—let me hide in the open. Now my eyes open.

VI. MORAL WARHORSE Make me cymbal. Make my brass turn blue. Future, I'm you. A little less fever and a little more war in my veins and gut. I would not shoot my former owner. I shot your former owner. Call me honor, not horror, out in the open. They killed Tom but not tomorrow. I still miss my Mama. So I need to be a hero. Must be. I'm blood-slow riot. I'm regiment. I'm soon-to-come religion. I'm road.

VII. THE FATHER CRIME Go back in time. Tell about the ones not ancient and not alive. Tell who lied. Pray, tell. European deities, barely belonging to each other, are restless, reckless, and aim to taste the Mississippi. Love, now. Change, now. Lie, now. Need. Hide the blood from the children. Love, keep the children in the dark—no, in the light—inside the plea that breeds the secret.

VIII. WHITE SHADOW Stay back, in time. Careful, cousin, lies are beautiful music. Black music. Believe me, cousin. Our land does not agree. Our law, our land. Choose wisely what you will call your country. We are not amused. We are full, so made more eager. I see you see where lies belong. You need not ask for what you already grasp, you own. This is only our home.

IX. GIVEN WHOLE Children, present in time. Notions made of time. Skin signatures. Blood thinks. Don't say difference is sin sickening my mind. My mind wars like a country. We diddle like countries. Flee what you can of this fervor. Remember, I never knew a home. The body's constitution is immythical, is unpeculiar. And yet, this Peculiar Institution. Your lips bury mine. Cover yours. Forever inside what I once owned.

X. INHERITANCE
Dear Cousin, I never lied. I will take. I will make mine. I will spend your children. I will make them honey or make them wine. Now I'm horizon line. Some will learn to die. Some will learn to fight. But this war, ancient? This war is just another and more fever.

XI. AMERICAN CIVILITY

Outside the body: We are two different people. We are too different people. We are two different people. Inside the body: We are two different people. We are too different people. We are two different people. We are too—   We do not believe in one.

XII. SPOIL Now, war over, they say this is my body. I had to go to see my former owner. She did not know how not to be my owner. I showed her. She will always be a miss to me. Where are the old ones that remained? Do they remember me? What will they make of my blue-uniform being? Do they still meet between the jagged trees, with secrets?

XIII. VOID You and I are searching for two different people. We will find and fall into Revival in a dark wood made of me, made for me. We bore into family. Our losses love each other. Your mother, my grandmother. Don't scare her. I am a violent dawn beyond my body. Can I not hide? I want to find what you found in the wood.

XIV. ECHO FOR GROUND Body between fear and faith, I make a kind of freedom. I make medicine with my mind. I find the things I need. I find and make and leave a long kind of family. No seeds have been given to me. I am not quite haven. I still need to run. I river up and down this country. I am eager. I break inside of night. Still, I.

DAVID GREENWOOD

A Little Place

Today, during lunch, or while *getting* lunch as they now say accurately enough, in line at one of the ready-made soup and sandwich places serving this cluster of offices, stood our giant!

Yes, sir, the eyes of another man, more a boy in a tie, sparked at me, *that is a seven-footer at least!* How could I explain?

I had seen him from the rear, the perilously high, delicate shoulders, the side of a cheekbone, and naturally the glimpse suggested our giant. But even if he were still by chance alive, would he be in this city sustaining himself on soup, when once you and I, crouched in the wood behind your father's store, saw him eat an entire layer cake out of the garbage bin?

After that, if a thin dog or even a squirrel came near and you grabbed my mitten, I would know you were about to say, "What do you suppose he's doing right now?" speaking dreamily of our giant. Then I would mutter something not very inventive, affected as I was with the peculiar anxiety one feels when meeting a departed friend in a dream, sensing his or her precariousness and not wanting to call attention to the trespass.

Advancing now through the soup-line maze, the huge man and I drew abreast, divided only by the nylon of the maze ribbon, the back of his clean-smelling shirt to the crown of my head. I could hear him sighing to himself, from impatience, it seemed, more than melancholy. Then he turned to look out the window.

It was our giant!

He was swart and craggy as ever—craggier, being older. What could I tell him? It wouldn't do to belt out however lovingly, "You were our giant!" I might rub my hands together, saying, as if unable to contain myself, "I see the pumpkin bisque is back, summer is really over!" But in my shyness I supposed he would see through this, or think I addressed him only for the novelty of addressing a giant, which must often happen and sadden him a little though he's used to it—or maybe no one talks to him for this fear, or some baser fear, just as you and I never spoke to him.

But then maybe he was the while containing his own surprise that I of all people should be here, and that he had the capacity, he could not help congratulating himself, to recognize me. How do we know somehow this is absolutely impossible?

He gave no indication, and anyway only the most gifted giant would recognize me after so long, so out of context, alone. The line advanced so that we were no longer neighbors, and I relaxed. I didn't have it in me to address him like a man of the world. Another moment and I might have spoken, not so much to him as through him, so to say, like a kind of megaphone, as if that way I could tell you, in this little place, ordering soup and half a sandwich, that with me even now stands our giant!

M. WEST

Ganzfeld, Los Angeles

So dark it was the dogs would not walk, not one of them
and our eyes spinning in their sockets
like the eyes of a someone in a cartoon
who has been hit, hard, and knocked over the side
of some steep cliff
suspended for a second as if gravity were another
option to choose from
candy store-style, licorice in bins, sticks of black
and red, soft jelly hearts and soft teeth
smelling like strawberry, tiny black tires
full of salt and hardness
spit out by the street until the sidewalk clicks when
you step on it.
The room was magic even if it was a museum made
to look that way,
colors soft and bright as blush,
lipstick and eyeshadow, cat collars, gems you stick all
over your face
and the colors changing that white room
and its annex every shade of pink, blue, orange, green
and gray,
the room rounded like candy and powdery-looking
but every object in the room, meaning other people,
perfect strangers, in sharp focus,
creases and eyelashes outlined and almost harsh
but the air diffuse and the doorway we climbed in
up the black steps also changing. All night
our eyes felt the light
of other places; the sharp blue dots on bar glasses
the chandeliers and their glow, even white plates
put forth a shine
as the black cod glistened in sauce; wine put a red shift
into the atmosphere

as if we were falling apart or flung distant from every
other object, just far enough to pull together
beneath a sign for dry cleaning and cars zipping past
our eyes open wide and white to catch the light.

NICHOLAS D. NACE

The Hundred Faults

> "There are an hundred faults in this Thing, and an hundred things might be said to prove them beauties."
> OLIVER GOLDSMITH

who
 who at that time
as we grow old
 with age
blood
 blood with us
or
 and others are smitten with
house
 house for the first time
beautiful
 dutiful
another daughter
 a daughter again
it is
 it would be
happiness
 utility and happiness
my favorite principle
 monogamy
our misfortune
 my misfortunes
lovers
 young lovers
had passed
 passed away
why then should not we learn to live
 and we are not so imperfectly formed as to be incapable
  of living

vanquished or victorious
  he rose or fell
its pleasures
  the pleasures it afforded
are still some men like you
  is still some benevolence left among us
to understand perfectly
  perfectly to understand
reverence
  reverence itself
falling
  shattered
we went
  he went
lofty strain
  one almost at the verge of beggary thus to assume
    language of the most insulting affluence might
    excite the ridicule of ill-nature
harmless
  innocent
retreat
  new retreat
was made
  we made
the children
  my children
guests
  other guests
after us
  after us for a show
this curtailing
  being thus curtailed
blank.
  blank. "But those," added I, "who either aim at
    husbands greater than themselves, or at the
    ten thousand proud prize, have been fools for
    their ridiculous claims, whether successful or
    not."

character
character among men
agreed
concluded upon
thirty
above thirty
holds
already holds
creation
nation
his assent
their reception
his errors
their incursions
so that
like corrupt judges on a bench, they determine right on
that part of the evidence they hear; but they
will not hear all the evidence. Thus, my son
faithless phantom
phantom only
modern
haughty
hour a mercenary
morn the gay phantastic
man
middle-aged man
deserve to possess
deserve
so well pleased
well pleased
again
now again
girl
girl, with a serious face
very tolerable figure
so contemptible
sound
swoon

enquiries
   enquiries more
wound. Upon which he cried out to his little
      companion. My little heroe
   wound, cried out to him. Come on, my little heroe
accuse
   punish by accusing
fifth
   fifth more impertinent than all the rest
my esteem
   all my esteem
following the purchaser, and having back my horse
   having back my horse, and following the purchaser
visage
   sweet visage
hackney'd
   favourite
few virtues they have
   shame at doing evil
imperfections
   defects
his uncle
   his rich uncle
not to be too frugal
   richly set
Whistonian
   Bangorean
family
   family in reality
could
   should
malicious
   ill-natured
resolved
   fixed upon
from
   since
resolution, in preferring happiness to ostentation
   resolution

Deborah
  Deborah, my dear
from the summits of pleasure, though the value
      of misery below may appear at first
  to the vale of wretchedness, which, from the
      summits of pleasure appears
brighten
  brighten, unexpected prospects amuse
interest
  seeming interest
with the rich
  among each other
governor
  tyrant
enemy over them
  the external enemy
pretended
  bold
have been
  have been once
Monogamy
  Hierarchical monogamy
obscurity
  unpitied obscurity
with the devotion of a monastic
  being dark, damp, and dirty
subsistence
  bare subsistence
the more
  still more
but with a proviso
  with this injunction
red
  was read
ninety-nine
  many
ever
  almost ever

ladies
ladies dressed in white
marry her to another in a short time
readily marry her to another
appeared
appeared as
got
gained
perpetration
perpetuation
beside
next
property
possessions
it
my last happiness that I have committed no murder,
tho' I have lost all hope of pardon
your lessons
the lessons
broken
woe-worn
sister, and who has five hundred pounds!
sister

GINA ABELKOP

We Love Venus!

Cackle cackle cackle We do! Lacing our greasy hands together We skip
down the street blowing raspberries on each other's cheeks leaving red and
purple stains there. We laugh, shove berries into our mouths pulled out
from neon plastic ziplock bags, laugh and the red spittle and purple spittle
and a little bit of blue spittle rains on the sidewalk in front of us and We
laugh and laugh and laugh! When We laugh too hard We run a little bit a
little ways ahead until We get the laughs out it makes us stop and focus on
running. And laughing!

   We have left the world behind and We are going to live on Venus. We
have bought our tickets with money We saved up working hard jobs for
dirty, stupid years in boring cities where everyone thinks they're funny
they're not funny they are our real enemies! Dumb blowholes stuffed fat and
sulky with all the stupid, inhumane facts of the world.

   Back to blowing bubbles We go at it, We blow big red bubbles at the
sky laughing seeing where Venus sits scary bright. You can hop a space
flight to one planet or another with a mask on filling your lungs full of
air and your space mask on making you look ugly and your space mask on
making you look smart or your space mask off, slowly strangling and finally
your lungs get sucked out into space without you and eventually hit the sun
and explode. Sorry lungs! But it did feel good to go out without your space
mask on the air in space, We hear, smells like cookies. Anyways on Venus
We need no masks it's set up for all good to go! Biodome alright!

   The letter came out only a month ago in the worldwide newspaper of
the deformed and dead-gone which is all of us, at this point, not We but all
of everyone else except We. ARE YOU DONE WITH EARTH DO YOU
WANT TO GO TO VENUS it asked. Yes We want to go to Venus We
screamed! We slapped each other with wooden spoons and blew raspberries
at our ugly neighbor and did a wild dance on our brown dried dead front
lawn to our favorite songs whose lyrics are something like "DANCE THE
SKIN OFF YOUR HEELS AND SQUISH THE BLOOD INTO THE
SIIIIIIDEWAAAAALK" which is a really good song to dance to, outside,
next to the sidewalk. We acted it out literally but cheated scraping our heels
on the sidewalk 'til they bled then hobbled on our heels chirping at the ugly

neighbor chirping at each other being really excited for We are going to Venus!

The first thing that must be done before We go to Venus is: sell our house. Our house is painted red, purple, and a little bit of blue and is shaped like a bigass donut, a round circle surrounded by an empty moat We filled with broken glass instead of water because most people these days can swim! And We don't want anyone trying to swim into *our* sweet donut! You enter through the triangle-shaped door (that's the little bit of blue) and you see, through the glass wall slobbered with lipstick and greasy handprints the interior of our donut, the center donut hole which is a garden We've decked out in every kind of flower that will grow in our dead-like city that is also red or purple: roses, slinky velvet violets, peonies, poppies, forsythia, wisteria, irises with goofy fluffy beards. There are garden stakes with artichokes slapped on top with googly eyes glued to them, the heads of our enemies! Bloodless representations for any who dare enter to see that WE! DO! NOT! FUCK! AROUND!

Who can We sell our donutty house to that would not offend us greatly by razing it to the ground to build a condominium housing one of our many enemies? We think about it for a while while We paint our nails one hand purple one hand pink one hand yellow one hand blue which We do by pouring the polish straight from the bottle onto each fingertip, plop plop ten times and then We have entire fingertips all dipped and colorful for weeks! So We do our nails and brainstorm and suddenly We think, Pansy! Pansy lives in a dog igloo she likes round houses! Pansy paints walls with confetti icing and smears it on the window "Hey y'all it's tinted windows!" she says! Sell the house to Pansy for the price of a dollar plus an original brand new just for us performance of which Pansy is always the genius queen! We pick up the phone with our still sticky nail polish fingers smearing our sheer pink plastic phone that has its electric guts glowing neon purple and call up Pansy:

"Hi Pansy howdee do!" We say.

"Hi howdee do-de!" says Pansy, We say,

"Will you buy our house Pansy?!" and she says, confidential-toned,

"You taking that first spaceship to Venus?" We says,

"Oh yeah!" Pansy replies,

"Oh *yeah!*"

and We've sold our house to Pansy! We tell her what We want in return: one dollar and a Very Special performance and Pansy comes over in an hour to perform for us. We ready the donut hole for her performance by lighting candles all around, candles We made from the beeswax of our ugly neighbor which We stole because fuck you ugly neighbor! The candles smell sweet like honey and We burn them, twenty or forty of them on top of the artichoke heads wax melting down into the googly eyes take that representations-of-our-enemies!

Bang bang bang Pansy knocks on our door and We run click-clacking in purple patent leather pumps to the door shrieking Pansy! Pansy! Pansy! Because We know she will be wearing the best outfit and she is. We open the door and Pansy is wearing short shorts made out of stretchy tight cheetah print fabric which she sewed herself into with thick red yarn criss-crossing at the sides and crotch like knotty, soft fresh scars. On top covering her ample tits Pansy wears a swath of musty-smelling black lace smeared with baby powder, tied in front like a bow with a big rhinestone bumble-bee brooch snapped on there how did Pansy know about our beeswax candles?! Tied into her hair hangs little ram's horns swinging around Pansy's shoulders with sequins glued haphazardly there too making them shine when they swung. Pansy's bare legs bore things she'd tattooed there herself with ink and needle, like every dinosaur ever discovered in dotty miniature, and We always like to lick the stegosaurus a little bit. It takes up the entirety of Pansy's left thigh it looks so good! And the other leg with a lion starting at her ankle and roaring yellow fire all the way up her pretty and thick cellulitey thigh— it took her forever to finish, like ten years of supremely patient stick-n-poke good job Pansy!

Pansy hugs us and makes her way to the donut hole where she will perform for us. Pansy's thermal-color plastic high heel mules are turning blue and then red and then pink as she click-clacks down the leopard print linoleum front hall. She licks a dollar bill and slaps it to the glass door where it sticks before she opens the door to set up her theatre outside. It's dark out by now and We can see exactly three stars in the sky but those three are super bright and they are next to Venus! Which has moved so conveniently close to the moon all by itself! The two of them sisters like We looking on each other in the sky is a good omen. Pansy sets out her costume: yards and yards and yards of synthetic hair macraméd together with shiny beads and fistfuls of hardened wax and bits of wilted, dirty rags. Pansy wipes electric blue stripes over her eyes with blue paint and Pansy laughs with her head thrown back and mouth to the sky and Pansy tells us to shush and then Pansy hitting the play button on her tape player begins:

She became Pansy-as-monster, dancing like a wild thing in her costume dangling dried pig ears and little silver horns. She brandished a knife and ground her fruit-bruised knees into our donut hole stage, her plastic-hair-hood removed to let out the dark bouncy curls and ram's horns, ice-eyes shadowed in bright blue doing their own kind of howling she cut apart a bundle of wax and hair. It wasn't a real baby her laughter said! She was inside herself totally performing that inside-ness for us and We could feel too her relief our relief at finding out the baby she killed wasn't at all a baby! We really felt and still feel that this was well worth the price of the best house in the city the donut house We sold to Pansy for a licked dollar and a dance *THANKS PANSY!*

We needed to get our stash our stash of money. We needed to move out move out of our donut house, clear the way for Pansy. We put on our moving outfits of stretch pink and purple ice-skating costumes and began making piles of needs and not-needs, what to take and what to burn in the spot designated for burning unwanted items in there We tossed:

Wigs and wigs and piles of wigs in purple, red, pink and a little bit of blue, our bed in the shape of sea shell in opalescent white our pink Kitchen Aid mixer our fifteen hula hoops our high heeled mules in every color our lipsticks in every color our fridge full of fake meats food-colored purple and red our knives with their abalone handles our collection of metallic nail polish our jewelry made of plastic and gold our artichoke enemy heads on stakes our beeswax candles our collection of porcelain sheep dogs left to us by our grandmother our dresses of which there's at least 100 last but not least our not unsubstantial hat boxes filled with hats all blue our dollar bill from Pansy and in the not-needs pile:

Thousands of frizzing balls of our real hair three hairbrushes ten pairs of matching bra and underwear sets our green wool couch with stuffing popping out of its many loose cracks two three-legged chairs dead plants by the millions dirty plates dirty saucers dirty tea cups full of mold. This We burned in the fire pit of our ugly neighbor who We tied to a tree while We used his pit ha ha! Our ugly neighbor cried and complained and We laughed and burned and burned. The burning hair smell rose into the air and even Pansy, pushing a little red wagon full of her waxy-haired not-babies, wrinkled her nose at the smell of our sour hairballs bursting into flames so We threw some roses from the donut hole at the burning pile and that sated everyone everyone but our true enemy our ugly neighbor who likes nothing We do, ha ha!

We look at our checklist what next? We must go purchase our tickets our tickets to Venus! We say Pansy can We get a ride and She says sure no problem get into my wagon. First she unloads the not-babies into her new home and then We hop in and Pansy pushes us all the way to the ticket office. On the way there Pansy sings to us a song she made up about being lost at sea. The lyrics went "Now I'm where I oughta be/lost at sea/now I'm where I oughta be/free in the sea/Now I can birth my baby/baby in the sea/I birth my baby free/free in the sea/cuz the sharks in the sea/they eat my baby/and the only way to be free/is a baby at sea/in the belly of a shark/along with my knees!" It was a really great song, pretty sad and moaning in an up-and-down way that sounded like the ocean waves nicely done Pansy! Pansy's back was to us and We had to agree, We had to say to Pansy You have a really great ass and she laughed and had to agree We all agreed on Pansy's ass.

·

People had begun giving birth to select limbs or body parts, often just a single, slippery organ. The most frequent cases were slimy eight-pound eyeballs, lumpy wet kidneys and rough, patchy tongues all streaked in the goo of birth when they slid out of the weeping pussies that bore them.

The kidneys and tongues were left on the labor table until they dried up, no longer emitting warm, soft livelihood; the emptied-out bodies of women carted off on stretchers, sobbing in fear and relief. While waiting for the tongues and kidneys to give their last lazy pulse of life doctors and nurses stood with their eyes down, silent.

It didn't matter if you were a doctor or a midwife or a doula or an aunt three times removed, you kept your mouth shut and your eyes lowered. It's called "non-denominational praying" and it's allegedly the most "human and respectful" way to handle this particular nightmare but trust us, We think decidedly not.

That didn't take long, maybe three or four minutes, the lonely dumped out tongues and kidneys gone hard and cold, mac and cheese left too long on a plastic dinner plate. Their mothers were encouraged to never set an eye or hand upon them, forget the whole mess entirely with a steady diet of woozy neon yellow pills that had the ripe side effect of giving you hyperreal dreams, which often had the side effect of making you piss and shit the bed you slept in, which was sometimes the stove or living room floor. Also recommended for their healing properties were soap opera distractions, but only ones that'd been running for going on hundreds of years. *As the World Turns, General Hospital*, plus a little known Sarah Michelle Gellar outfit called *Swan's Crossing* which We used to watch in the mornings before school when We were elementary, having spent the night at one or the other's house and splitting a packet of the pink-flavored Pop Tarts our mothers bought for us. These were the great national treasures, relatively concise histories of the American psyche.

The dumpy organs were discarded like cancerous tumors or breast tissue, flushed into the center of the earth where they begin to sizzle mid-way, bearing frighteningly close to that fire-hot core glowing at the exact center 'til they settled somewhere into the layer of bony sediment to which We'll never have access. These things couldn't live—you couldn't even transplant them into the sick bodies that needed tongues and kidneys. Their life was short, shorter by far than a mayfly's, and what could you do but accept it, because it was so.

The eyeballs, though, were a different story altogether, a Hans Christian Andersen tale so deeply and foreverly disturbing it made every kidnapping-rapist horror film look like a pastel-filtered Disney affair.

Those who were piously led into their Twilight Zone eyeball horror show lived nine months with little, and then not-so-little, eyes in their uteri. What this meant, long term, was that a gnarly pet lived out its seemingly endless days with you and your beloveds. They didn't grow, or mature, other than forming cataracts after 40 or 50 years. They'd hum along, silent, alive, and staring, for a regular human lifespan. Sitting in a box in your living room, blinking for decades, what We'd call *mildly sentient*. Long eyelashes matted together unless you brushed them with an extra large eyelash brush at least once a week, which by the way also cost at least three times what a regular comb does which is such a rip. The bootleg versions you could buy on the internet for cheap were just as good, but obstetricians always talked the big virtues of the official products and, you know, those poor-ass souls with eyeballs for offspring lapped that shit up, hungry for something Right and Proper to be attached to the whole mess. Cleaning the crust that gathered at the lash lines' phlegmy edges every day was a very real kind of care. Someone had to do it, and no, there weren't usually ugly stepsisters there to do the work but yes, sometimes there were, and they were inevitably exploited. Some families had two, three, even eight of these sightless suckers. Birth deformities didn't stop people from artificial insemination, which ended up in multiple eye-fetuses 34% of the time. The foster care systems nationwide were doing the best they ever had, placing teenage people in homes where the families would actually be very kind and generous, but also tell you that the one condition of being their beloved new family member rested upon these teenage people's ability to care for the shoulda-never-been-borned fuckin' eyeballs. And that's considered a healthy kindness.

Eyeball abortion wasn't an option, philosophically, economically, or logistically, for many women. News stories would cycle in and out, women performing abortions on themselves or each other because one of the two clinics left in the country either couldn't admit them in time or were too far away to make an affordable journey of it. Ten women would be on the news in a week, dead from septic pussy syndrome, aka the whole planet having had a worst-case-scenario makeover: Lookee Ma, we're a real live hell on earth! Consciousness raising groups were working hard to offer safe at-home abortion tips for the masses but, you know, not everyone has access to their booklets, their flyers, their organized kinda-doctors running sneakily through big city streets at 2 a.m., Jane 200.0. The thick gray air poisoned the appropriated medical tools as soon as they left their scratched plastic cases, which in turn poisoned your body and sometimes, despite our best latex-gloved intentions, everything just went to shit, shit and shit and shit and shit. Of course the news cycle ran these stories on a loop.

Don't die! Birth your eye!

The eyes, the eyes! They went on and on with their rudimentary self-sustaining system. You could bear them, if you could bear them. All God's creatures, blank staring not-babies pulsing along in your home, never saying nothing, just staring, reminding you that your whole body was just poison ricocheting off the atmosphere and laughing at you. Understandably, people started losing it, hacking their birthed eyes with steak knives, throwing them into the street in pulpy wet masses. Conservative, high-horsed eyeball-lovers with mean hearts would spray a big red eye on your front door and bury the eye in one of their mass eyeball graves. Tiny absurd headstones, all tear-stained plots eventually growing daisies or dahlias, whose seeds were dropped in during the large group funerals. Using flowers to shame people struck us square in the gut: an appropriation of some kind of natural joy flipped into a finger pointing brightly at all the traumatized. The country looked more and more like a massive cemetery conceived by a cruel, sadistic version of those singing *Alice in Wonderland* flowers, all lined up to mock you with their beauty. Nobody liked to see daisies or dahlias anymore. All they meant were poison and gore and sad people and the distinct sense of finality floating around whatever concept was left of human decency.

There were women's therapy groups that dealt specifically with these unfortunate birth-based traumas; therapists were making good money despite how little money seemed to be circulating. To make someone carry and birth something like a large slug and then expect them to just get on with it, therapist in firm-gripped tow. Even worse, companies dedicated solely to building small chambers for the eyeballs who weren't hacked or aborted, Barbie dream houses in gendered pink or blue satins and silks on which to plop mama's ugliest emission.

God made tongues! God made kidneys! God made plastic and bleach and chemicals and every single everything! God made the poison drifting aimlessly through the atmosphere, curly-q'ing into your nostrils and earholes and eyeball nooks! God made dicks filled with sick sperm filled with sick cells who'd tell your lonely masochistic eggs to do the wrong things, cook up the wrong dinner, lead your eggs down the bad, bad roads.

So We understand why women were leaving the planet in hoards. 94% of those warm bodies getting loaded onto the proverbial Venus train were women, women with warm, sick bodies that couldn't take it anymore. We don't wanna live here either! We wanna hop on the nearest truck headed for wherever, forever, and under pretty much any circumstance that, at the very least, promised complete physical separation from the planet that had done this to you.

A few months ago We sat on the toilet with wicked bad cramps and ended up pushing out a little tadpole of a quivering eyeball-ette. Still gummy and soft, with only a few short eyelashes and a translucent white film over the face, like a raw egg with a weepy iris in the middle. Could've fit fifteen of them at least on the palm of our hands, but there was only one. We remember, and consider, that rare encounter. Not, like, such a tragedy for us. We didn't want a baby, we hadn't even known We were incubating one. We didn't think to check. We're like that: letting life work it's own way through the body, out the first available hole, flushed down the toilet. It'd never happened to us before. But of course We imagined what would've happened if We'd grown up with the wrong people, with our true enemies, who are tricky and could get us to do whatever whatever just to give them a little something to smile all rotten-gummed about. We don't do that anymore— you better believe! But everyone's young once, so long as they're born with an appropriate selection of body parts. Not just one crummy piece.

.

Sometimes We take our heads off and trade with each other. When We were younger, cellulite still little cauliflower nubs undulating in our blood streams, We'd wake up in the middle of the night, poke our fingers in each other's stomachs and groggily switch heads mid-dream. When We woke up in the mornings We'd discuss how our bodies felt different or the same, how it changed the dream even though the dream was being dreamed in the same head the whole time, just with a different body beneath it. If a dream picked up where We left off, from before the head exchange, it'd usually take an abrupt turn right away. So We'd melt back into the narrative—maybe a beach where We were pulling seaweed out of the shallow surf while someone who didn't look like our mother but was our mother looked on—and all of a sudden a whale or long-lost friend would appear and shoot us in the face and We'd start a new tale altogether. Don't you always wonder about how you can't die in dreams, like even if you die you still have consciousness? You just move on to a different scene—cut!—the worst art film ever made because trying to explain it is like describing color without using any color words whatsoever to a person who's never seen a single color before. We played this game once, and it didn't work because We have four working eyeballs between us. We said, "Like a girl flower, velvety, the color of meat" and We'd answer, "red." Duh. We weren't learning anything new with these experiments, only trying to see if We could trick our minds into misunderstanding, or re-understanding, basic concepts like color and texture. You know—playing.

After We moved away from the coast and into foothills—from one city to another—We traded heads less often. It seemed useless. We knew each other's bodies well enough that it didn't make for anything interesting or stupid or fun anymore. We had a brother when We were kids who told us that some people can exchange fingers and toes but are fairly certain, at this late stage, that this isn't actually possible, though We haven't left the state ever, so have no clear idea of what's really "out there" any more than We have any idea of what's waiting for us on Venus. Besides a big rough canister of planet all empty and quiet, waiting to be filled with sloppy rocks and gravel like We.

You're well aware of the survival narrative. It basically goes: relative comfort, horror, horror, horror, near death, triumph, marginal comfort, horror, horror, and finally either death or living out the rest of your days all silent and nervy from all the horror. Men get to have their honor and ethics because they cheated the odds, more or less—even if they die, no other man's gonna call them a pussy. Maybe they'll have a wife who isn't as good as the dead wife from before but she's dedicated and thankful that someone would have her after all of *her* horror and that's basically where the family situation lays in this nation. When it comes to survival narratives.

If you've never switched your own head—which you really should have, everyone started doing it in elementary school and even the cryingest kids did it eventually—then you don't know that the best part, after synching up your brain with someone else's muscles, is the goopy suction sound that happens when you twist that sucker off. Sluuuuuuuuuurp schwoooooooooop !pop! it goes, and all of that so very wetly. Then you stick your head onto the new body and the sound goes shhhhhwwwwwwwwomp mmmmmmmmm. Some people hate it so much it makes them vomit instantly, and those people switch heads once or twice and then give it up entirely. We don't know, it got so casual, you'd switch heads with your true enemy if you found yourself playing on the playground with them, trusting they'd give it back, which they always did because who wants your dumb old head with its psoriasis on the scalp and greasy spots, smelling like whatever shampoo your mom could afford?

WILL SMILEY

Max Pengall's Christmas Story

There was a tremor
As in San Francisco
Or Lisbon. And Pengall
Watched as the
Dust shook him upward
To the heavens
From his cradle.

They'd said they'd mow
All the lawns (a
Figure in their speech
For death itself)
Before he bearing up
Could reach apples.

The shaking that had
Shaken him came and went
Again. He stood.
Stirred a muscle at a time
Until (this time)

He saw the adult remains
Of the two towns
Gripping the coastal hills.
Pengall mused on the girls
He loved there: his mother.
And his real mother
Giving birth to him.

CARMEN GIMÉNEZ SMITH

from "Post-Identity"

.

the animal   imagines   what life is   in her fiefdom
what the edges of her domain are
what parables   become policy
vice versa the animal   susses out   confederate
from the horde   the animal defines the age's pathology
how   will the   animal cure it
how does the animal describe   worry
and recognizing it   how does the animal
solve   the animal   outside of   time
does the animal become an immunity
or serve   the fiefdom   what is the give
and   the take away   is it false hope
inescapable class   the trap a fortress
we all grew up frozen   at a slant
are we up or down are we over
and out can we clamber in from the wilds

.

how shall we remind
the mathematicians
the politicians
and the statisticians
and the tax exempt
megachurch man
and the house flipper
and the executive garbage
who hiked up the cost
of Daraprim and EpiPen
and the complicit Ponzi
scheme of lobbyists
and the propogandists
and the Democrat-corporate
shills and the patriarchal
misogynist statesmen
how shall we reiterate
that want is drug is conduit
and capital is the rabies
impulse is the mechanism
nationalism the mask
the matrix is us sheeple
and so we should capture
the mike post-haste we're tired
of getting jostled on currents
dismissed by the judges
made into sex object
unwillingly reduced into
effigy or dismembered
on borders and razed
by the American appetite
for Sinaloan meth in teeny
baggies with skulls on them
each skull a human head
tossed to the furrowed canals
edging our border lined
with the bodies of journalists

and mayors a magical realism
not seen in your ethnic literature
will someone listen and if so
how will there be reparation
will it be animal mineral
or vegetable will it have
only symbolic heft and flavor
or will it be forcibly removed
will Nero hear from
his driverless chariots
with seats that lean back
into giant palanquins
shouldered into the sublime
to a condo on Mars
by rows and rows of bodies
not just brown but all our
bodies consumed by mythologies
of difference of disruption
will they listen
with respect with the republic
how will they feel when it's
explained and it's not feelgood
ribbon business but our
bodies like chattel in pens
because of the venerated
cannibal factory feeding
infinite and wanton wants
the pliancy of adolescence
bones sugar fecal matter silicone
gristle even cells broken down
into individual patents
the factory releasing
only one xenotype at a time
free with purchase of one
million shiny objects
shall we write our demands in blood
shall they be inscribed in the annals
of art and history
how do we transform their powers

do we break them apart and bury them
set them on the shelf
do we push them out
on the ice floe or take
away their scepters
can we disrupt it
with our word parades
do we extend ourselves
into walls again do we
let them in on the plot
or do we burn them

.

is my lineage apropos
my diction mid-to-high
is this the office where I turn
in my papers where I turn
on the reader did you examine
my permit my creed will I be
scorned or feted or disregarded
or memed or made to confess
and will I have to get christlike
will it be messy because I resisted
will you levee around
that flourish will you tighten
the reins or is this a limping treatise
often I hardly capture I'm doing
harpy that I'm a city's pestilence
but also the cure I'm under
and down but still tell-all
so do I thank you when you touch
my idiom do I mother or write
serve art or the state do I beg
you to power the engine
construct the proper institution
or is it a collective effort
one in which we feel noble
and broadcast our dignities
in the end do we take
it on singularly or as one bodily
force and is there a syntax
I can appropriate
for my limited parlance
or have I already done so
and no one has told me
because I am not
of their denomination

.

why are we wedged   so much so horchata
mulatta corbata pirata   and obvi piñata
metiste la pata   cuando abriste la boca
pero te lo digo with love

DAVID HOLLANDER

A Complete Picture

The fact of his inconsequentiality had not dawned in tiny increments the way it does for most humans, but swept through him all at once like an eclipse. He was with his father, aboard one of the last of the New York Central's steam-powered railcars on a sightseeing daytrip that would take them north along the Hudson and into Round Rock Hill where the father intended to show the boy an architectural anomaly, a "round" house recently built by a well-known and portly comedian that the boy was imagining (i.e., the house) as a *sphere* in which the comedian might roll around like some sort of enormous Weeble. The train thundered Godlike through many small Hudson Valley hamlets, one of which the boy would later in life call home though in his Manhattan youth the very idea of relocation was equated with surrender by parents whose confidence in urban liberalism's capacity to ward off Meaninglessness was total. The boy and his father were playing what they called *The Question and Answer Game*, in which each posed in turn a question to the other with points scored for "stumping" your opponent, and while the father of the boy limited his Qs to the likely scope of his (prodigal, or so the father liked to say) boy's breadth of knowledge, the boy had no choice but to go all in, cultivating his Qs from the most esoteric factoids yet unearthed here in his 12th year, and nothing was more satisfying than stumping the old man even if the boy suspected that his father was on those rare occasions feigning ignorance so as to make it all a little more fun for them both, like for instance did his father really not know that Pluto was the smallest planet in the solar system, or that squids had ten arms, or who wrote *Charlotte's Web*?, but it didn't matter because it was true that scoring a point here and there made it more Meaningful, and if his father was faking, it was generous in a way that the boy appreciated (it was the *idea* of befuddling the old man that mattered), and whenever his father would pause with real or assumed uncertainty, a finger raised to his stubbly chin, the boy's heart would thump fast and hard in his bony chest. For a 5th grader the boy thought a lot about Meaning. What was even stranger was that he *knew* he thought a lot about it … he knew he was different in some strange and not necessarily good way and already feared adulthood, when he would no longer have as a failsafe his ability to *please*, which ability he knew was integrally connected to the ephemeral happenstance of his being a child. He'd recently discovered in one of his father's textbooks something called "theodicy," which as far as he could tell was a kind of religious inquiry into why bad things happened to good people. Sometimes he would have nightmares in which God chased him down an ever-narrowing corridor. The deity was dressed in long white robes and wielded a bayonet. He shouted things like, "I am unhappy with our current arrangement!" or "This is not what I ordered!" On this particular bright afternoon the boy had the window seat. The river was being whipped by a fierce wind into a dangerous stucco and the mountains rose from the far shore radioactive with sunlight. Something about it all seemed frantic and worried. His father had just Q'd him a multiple choice: what is the distance between the earth and the moon?, and the boy had already excluded one of three choices, 93 million miles, which he knew (from a Q earlier that week) was the distance between earth and sun, and he tried to extrapolate the correct answer from the incorrect one while searching his father's face for clues. Sometimes the father took the boy with him to the college where he taught Political and Social Philosophy to smart-sounding young men (and a handful of young women, too) who called his father Professor Kitchen or in a few cases simply "Jake," which he wasn't sure which was weirder. The boy called his father "Daddy" and felt none of the embarrassment that some of his peers seemed to feel around their own parentals. In fact the boy felt nearly immune to all of the prepubescent embarrassment that seemed to haunt the other boys at his school basically 24/7. These classroom visits not only revealed to the boy that he could hold his own, intellectually speaking, among teenagers; they also taught him that his father was loved and respected by people other than he and his mother which epiphany the boy registered *as such*, aware that he was able to see his parentals as actual human beings and that he thus possessed a broader perspective than most boys his age which he additionally realized was pleasing to his parents so that he began remarking upon his own special variety of maturity whenever and however organically possible, so that (e.g.) when the boy and his parents would pass by a disobedient child the boy might say something like, "I don't think that guy's developed a very mature perspective," or "I feel so lucky to be beyond all of that, thanks to my perspective," and although some small part of the boy recognized that he would eventually be required to separate from and possibly even despise these parents, he was happy— here on the train that hugged the river that ran for the sea in crests of white frosting—to put that eventuality off for a little while longer and to make Meaning from the love that was either unconditional or else uni-conditional, because he suspected the love might well be contingent upon his ability to please them and confirm their sense of themselves as excellent and progressive childrearers, which if this was the case he didn't mind, it was a game he could play and excel at and it gave him pleasure to be its master.

He knew the speed of light and also he remembered that light from the moon's disc took roughly a second to reach his own eyes and so he knew the answer now but he didn't respond immediately because he wasn't sure what would please his father more in this instance, a correct or incorrect re-sponse. Still, the thrill of sudden understanding blazed up in him. It was his favorite feeling. The train veered briefly eastward to follow what appeared to be an enormous bite-mark in the shoreline and with this slight change in angle sunlight exploded through the window to illuminate his father's face, the deep wrinkles around his eyes. His father wore a blue button-down shirt and blue jeans and the train's seats were blue. The sky outside the window sustained the idiom, a pale blue canvas on which the mountains were paint-ed crudely and in anger. "Time's up," his father said. The boy read the clues in his face and decided he would utter the incorrect answer. He was just opening his mouth when the brakes screamed and the train lurched wildly forward. Its bones seemed to buckle. Passengers grabbed at seatbacks in an effort to steady themselves as the event moved into that strange stop-time that the boy would later learn was characteristic of traumatic events. The train finally whiplashed to a rest and something settled deep inside its belly and the boy realized his father was holding his (the boy's) bicep very tightly. He looked down at the cracking skin of the old man's knuckles and at the thick silver wedding band that seemed incongruous with the warmth of human bodies. Meanwhile facts were registering. They were between stations. No platform was in sight. The shore of the Hudson River was only fifteen or twenty feet away and the enormity of the train seemed to the boy suddenly ridiculous, the idea of putting a hundred tons of steel in such close proximity to water suggesting an almost pathological confidence, and just as he was about to tell his dad that he was all right, *You can let go of me now Daddy*, the conductor's voice arrived as if from heaven to inform them—in the same kind of controlled panic that he associated with the flustered bay-onet-wielding God of his dreams—that there was something on the tracks and they would be held in their current position until it could be attended to and that as soon as he had more information he'd share it. *Sorry for the inconvenience and thank you for riding the New York Central Railroad.*

Disembodied authority seemed to calm everyone, including the father, Jake Kitchen, who released the boy's arm unbidden and chuckled at his own fear. "That was interesting, huh Tom?" he said. "I wonder what's out there." Walls were beginning to fall inside the boy. Many of the adults were lighting cigarettes, theorizing on everything from a stalled vehicle to a teenager's prank. The train's size was somehow more real without motion. So much *material*. And yet of course it was not unique. There were thousands of trains. Maybe hundreds of thousands. All that iron ore melted down to fashion miles and miles of cumbersome steel panels that might keep inside and outside safely dividered.

The boy now noticed that there was a kayaker out on the water. The kayaker was not paddling. In fact his paddle rested against the front ridge of his seat. Or not his seat . . . his hole, the boy thought. He is a man sitting in a hole floating in the river. The kayaker was leaning forward and his mouth was slightly agape, his profile aglow with sunlight and the other side of his face presumably cooler and in darkness. The river was rough but the kayaker's expensive-looking gear gave him away as a man who could do some serious paddling, plus he was basically hugging the shore so as to avoid the worst of the Hudson's notoriously unforgiving currents. What the boy realized was that the man on the water could see what had happened, why the train had stopped. Which meant that, in a certain way, he too—the boy Thomas Kitchen—could also see what had happened, if only through the kayaker's eyes. He made in his mind a triangle between himself, the man, and the third thing. They were each connected and each relied on the others for a fuller understanding of the event. The kayaker knew what the train had hit; the boy knew the feel of the lurching train and of his father's grip marks burned into his bicep; the thing on the tracks (and the boy already knew in his gut that they had not hit a *thing*, they had hit a *person*) knew what it was to be vaporized by a dispassionate machine. No single perspective could yield the entire experience, but taken together these points in the triangle created something strong and solid. "Tom?" his father was asking. "Do you see something?" The boy could smell something vaguely floral, his father's deodorant maybe, activated by stress. Or else maybe some shaving product. Also he could smell gasoline and something burnt or burning.

"Daddy?" the boy said. He was going to ask, *"What will it feel like to die?"* But he didn't. He felt suddenly as if he already knew. A partial death was already inside him.

They waited in the warm, close air of the unmoving train for more than an hour, the cigarette smoke of strangers collecting at the top of the

car like a storm system as curiosity gave way to irritation, the sun all the
while gliding slowly toward the mountains like some doomsday device of
unimaginable scale set to detonate on contact with those stony peaks, the
conductor periodically assuring them that shuttle buses were on their way
and would remove them to points further north (the new rail hub of Croton
Harmon was only several miles from their current position) where trains
would be available for travel in either direction. The boy's father spoke with
adjacent passengers whose own suppositions about their journey's sudden
interruption fluctuated between the two poles of disaster and disaster avert-
ed, their voices growing hushed there in the presence of the boy who was
all the while calculating. When their shuttles did arrive—a fleet of yellow
school buses no doubt commandeered by municipal authorities—the passengers were helped one by one from open doors down to the track several
feet below, Jake Kitchen preceding his boy to earth and then turning to take
his son in his arms and gently lower him down. The driver of the bus was
a large man with thick skin whose sincere smile and gentle mannerisms
further confirmed the presence of death. Many years later the boy would be
a man and would press his face to a window that resembled a ship's porthole
to catch glimpses of the wife who lay under the spell of general anesthesia
within a cyclone of attending physicians while her womb was sliced open to
spit forth the daughter within, and although he would not be permitted entrance into that bloodletting chamber he would be afforded brief moments
of eye contact with a surgeon upon whose masked face the man would find
himself superimposing this bus driver's, which was how he would know
(with his face pressed against the porthole) that someone would die. Either
the child he did not know or the woman he knew and loved. And Death
would not be in a bargaining mood and would not (as he begged Him to)
take the child and spare the wife, and two days later he would drive home
with the little girl Grace and two days after that bury his wife in the cold
wet earth of early March under a sun that shed no heat with the bus driver's
face everywhere. Now though, as he climbed aboard the bus as an 11-year-
old boy, he registered only the fact that the driver knew things he (the boy)
did not about the contours of the event. In the same way that he could
connect his perspective to the kayaker's and then to the victim's to create a
fuller rendition of a particular moment in space-time, he could now connect his experience aboard the screeching train to this driver who had been
called unexpectedly to duty by whatever official had likewise been roused
to action by a phone call, the driver possessed of certain data that would
further develop the picture of the event but could not complete it. The boy's

father ushered him to a window seat and pulled a brown paper bag from the same leather satchel he used to cart class materials to and from the college where he was so respected. Inside the bag were an apple and a banana. He held them both out. The boy took the apple and held it in his palm, feeling its weight. How far had it come to arrive here? What was its story? The bus took off and circled the parking lot before entering traffic, providing the boy with a view of various emergency vehicles: firetrucks, police cruisers, ambulances, their various sirens spinning and weakly strobing beneath the sun's glare. He thought about his *perspective*. You could draw a line between himself and the kayaker, then to the conductor who saw the body explode, then to the driver of the bus, then to his father there beside him peeling a banana, then home to his mother who would in another hour or two hear them pushing through the front door of the apartment on Columbus Avenue far earlier than expected, they having abandoned the idea of viewing Jackie Gleason's round house (which in later years the words "round house" would make Tom Kitchen laugh like a man possessed) after so much waiting and tedium… you could draw all these lines and you would have a fuller picture of something. But of what? What if you knew what everyone in Manhattan knew? Everyone in the United States? Everyone on earth? What would the complete picture be a picture *of*?

The boy's brain tingled. He was 11 years old. He had a life ahead of him, or he suspected as much, though he knew in that moment that it was never going to make any more sense to him than the very limited kind of sense it made right then. The unfortunate boy was seized by the unfortunate certainty that this, *this* moment, was the peak of intuition, from which all else was descent.

He watched his father bite into the banana. *Nobody cares*, he thought. *No one knows anything and nobody cares.*

"It's 'B'," he said aloud. "200,000 miles."

From the novel-in-progress Anthropica.

MARTY CAIN

THE VALUES BY WHICH MEN HAVE FOUND IT POSSIBLE NOT
MERELY TO SURVIVE BUT TO LIVE WITH DIGNITY

That thing I call the Death Apparatus: that thing I call the Swallower
of Life: that thing which says *The library is closing* in its languid voice
adrift from the intercom, which lines us up by the door & holds a gun to
our unblinking eyes, which sees INDETERMINATE LIGHT & quivers
& triggers our skulls into moss, which has spun blankets from unwhite
flesh hung like a beacon from its balcony in the square: which makes a
white square with its membrane of knives: which believes in frames with a
membrane of knives: which lines bodies lengthwise upon each street, which
marks in ink its favored parts: which drools upon its favored parts: which
keeps in the kitchen closet its favored parts: which with proper technique
saws open its favored parts: which one day eats the corpse of the young
with the apple in its mouth & toasts its goblet to the chandelier: which
says *We've done it boys we've really done it*: which sees no blood from the
chandelier: which knights itself as Accountable Fairness: which identifies
with the bird it is swiftly killing: which refers to its daughter as its God-
Given Pony: which eats its turkey & falls asleep on the couch with the TV
light on its meaty fingers: which wakes up shivering with its meaty fingers:
which the next day alurch from the shower pukes upon its bathroom rug
& washes fast its meaty fingers: which gets in its Lexus: which gets in its
Mazda: which gets in its Prius: which gets in its Landrover: which turns
on the seat heater & waits at the light: which sweats a dark death from its
venerable hole: which turns the brightness swiftly down, for every screen is
afire today: which says GOOD EVENING which tramples unfed faces on
linoleum floors: which tramples unfed faces at a midnight sale for the flat
screen for the rifle for the Large-Size Pool for the leather boots polished
with the trampled faces staring back: which stares in the mirror & speaks
to itself: which says *I am no abuser* which says *I have several small demands*
which says *I have learned to live like this*: which has drank its young within
its frames.

ELIZABETH CLARK WESSEL

Carol and Shirley

almost every day Carol visits Shirley or Shirley visits Carol
when Shirley is sick Carol visits Shirley when Carol is sick
Shirley visits Carol These are the people that have died
in car wrecks the four teenagers, the one teenager, the toddler
who took his tricycle onto the highway survived but then died
of a heart attack his parents died in car wrecks the mother
of Julia died in car wrecks the brother of Sam had a wife
and a son who drown and her father drown too and then his other
son almost died in a car wreck but no one else of that family has
died yet and the two children who died in the electrical fire
and the child that was shot by the other child When Shirley is
sick Carol visits when Carol is sick Shirley visits These are
the couples who cheated the banker's wife across the street and
the lawyer and the man who owned the trailer park had two women
at home can you believe it and the one who died golfing she put
his golf clubs on the sidewalk and in the bag is the blanket to be used
as a table cloth and the magazines about Diana and the picture frame
and the headband and the gently used socks The people that have died
of cancer are the other Shirley the first Shirley Shirley visits Carol visits
Shirley visits Carol These are the people they have known These are
the people who have died after living These are the organism These are the
good bacteria These are the close calls and the visits of Carol and of Shirley

DIANA CAGE

Illustrations by Buzz Slutzky

The Husbands

I was at the Metrograph, a new movie theater on Ludlow Street, when a woman approached me in the lobby. "Can you fucking believe this?" she said. I nod just to be nice until I realize she's performing that faux shock that long time inhabitants of formerly crummy New York neighborhoods love so much. She is right though; the theater is over the top. There was a guy in the lobby dressed exactly like Marlon Brando in *On the Waterfront*, and Ted and I split a twelve-dollar bottle of green juice before the film. We watch a documentary on Fassbinder that's mostly mediocre. After, at Congee Village, I tell my friends the story of watching *The Bitter Tears of Petra Von Kant* while having sex with my then husband for the last time.

Petra tells a story about falling out of love with her husband. She's putting on makeup, fawning over her own beauty while sensuously stroking the fur trim on her white satin gown. Suddenly she turns and forcefully pins her friend Sidonie to the bed. Petra lies on top of Sidonie and describes the disgust she felt during sex. She has some gems in this monologue, describing his filthy smell—"He stunk of man,"—and her reluctant submission—"He mounted me like a bull mounts a cow," she tells her Sidonie, "with no regard for a woman's pleasure." Sidonie lies dead-eyed on the pillow while Petra goes on about the shame she felt when she orgasmed beneath him.

"At that point I started crying," I explain to everyone at the table.

I'd been dating a woman named Karen for weeks while trying to stay married to Ian, and they were both about to break up with me. Crying after sex is fine, but crying during is not a good sign.

Fifteen years later Ian is breaking up with someone else and maybe I am too. He's laughing at me because I don't understand how Tinder works.

"But sometimes I get notifications that say, 'You have new people interested in you.' So I click to see who liked me."

Ian used Tinder all the time and had hoarded a list of matches, which I now understood were women who he'd liked who'd then liked him back. He never contacted any of these women, but he often visited the list, satisfied by its potential.

"How is your sex life?" my cool new doctor asked. "Are you monogs?"

Discussions of monogamy are now so ubiquitous we don't even use the whole word. JMill asked if I was nonmono—like a test result. I can't help it. I only want to fuck my husband. What happened? When I lived in San Francisco, every party turned into an orgy, totally normal. Not so in New York. Last Christmas, Max and I were cruised by a famousish academic. Should we have a threeway with her? I was very worried about the details. Who would do whom? Would it be gauche to bring her to the apartment on the subway? Do I need to clean the bedroom? By the time we were done discussing the idea, the subject had left town.

My cousin Bets reaches for me, her face screwed up and red. Why the sobbing? I wonder. I haven't seen her in ten years. She looked different then, long hair, very normal. She mumbles sympathetically while gripping my shoulders so that I hunch uncomfortably forward. I silently urge her to release me before I have to say something and make it awkward. She feels small in my arms. I think I must feel large in hers. Everyone I like tells me that frailty isn't attractive but I don't believe it.

Bets was my mentor when we were kids. She taught me everything— how to roll joints, how to chop up drugs for snorting. She took me to concerts and taught me what an eighth of weed and an eight ball of cocaine should look like. She used her mom's kitchen scale, which usually heaved under piles of millet from the bulk bin, to parcel out bricks of weed into baggies to be distributed among the boys at our high school. The girls were interested only in Adderall, which Bets also supplied, having had a prescription since childhood.

"Bets," I say, as meaningfully as I can manage as my father's funeral drags on. "I have such a headache. Do you have anything I can take?" Is she high? Why is she crying? I feel conspicuous asking for pills, like a tragic lesbian on the cover of a pulp novel. She finds ibuprofen in her purse, a little foil packet like you buy in bodegas. I'm too embarrassed to ask her for Vicodin, so I take the packet and slip it into my pocket. No one in California takes drugs anymore.

My dad's girlfriend has the urn tucked into the crook of her arm. The design, the funeral director said, would prevent "ash blowback." Ash blowback sounded like something I wanted to avoid. I once helped Ian scatter the ashes of his friend Ray in the park where he used to cruise for sex. Ashes are heavier and chunkier than you'd expect. They stick to your fingers, which you will inevitably wipe on your jeans like Cheetos. And then there's wind. Huge gusts blew bits of Ray into our faces, where they stuck to my lip gloss.

"This funeral cost more than a wedding," Candy said, stuffing the urn into a tote bag and putting it in the trunk. She wanted to get married, but my father put it off. "You already have a ring," he told her. And what a ring, I think, as I stare at her glinting hand. It's enormous. A giant cushion-cut diamond, set in yellow gold, highlighted by her long, elegant fingers and ballet slipper colored manicure. I get a lot of pleasure out of her earnest femininity. I was married to Ian for ten years. I wore his clothes. Straight men love a pretty version of themselves.

Ian and I married on a whim and were dismayed when the clerk explained that we needed a ceremony to make it legal. So fortunate that many of our friends were ordained by made-up churches. This was pre-internet, when you found out about things like ordainment in the back pages of *Rolling Stone*. A pagan demi-goddess married us on her rooftop. We threw a party, scrambled up a ladder to the roof-access billboard, and made it legal in front of a picture of two smiling, white-toothed smokers holding a pack of Parliaments.

When Max got a job in California and I decided to stay in New York, I wanted to get married. I imagined marriage as a magical force that would tether us to each other. Why I would think this, I can't explain. I wanted, especially, a ring, which seemed like a talisman. Max was bewildered and refused to play along with my fantasy. "I don't believe in marriage," he said. Adding, in case it wasn't clear, "I don't want to be married."

Roland Barthes says that missing a lover is a woman's problem. Men leave and women write about it. To miss someone, he says, is to become feminine. I wonder now if Max's refusal to marry me was more about gender. Were we a lesbian couple? Maybe he didn't want to be my wife. How can I possibly unravel something as mundane as this? My therapist said, "You identify as a lesbian." I wasn't sure where she was going. And then, in a gentle, concerned tone, she said something so mortifying I cringe in recollection. "Since you are a lesbian, would you rather be with a *woman*?"

Oh boy. In my mind I thought, "Lady, I have never dated a woman in my entire lesbian life." No one is homophobic anymore. I mean, sure, bakeries in the Midwest don't want to make gay cakes, but otherwise straight people are down.

"Well, I suppose I've stopped thinking about sexual identity," I told her. "I am a lesbian because that is how I identify culturally but not because I think 'man' and 'woman' are actually discrete categories." Who knows

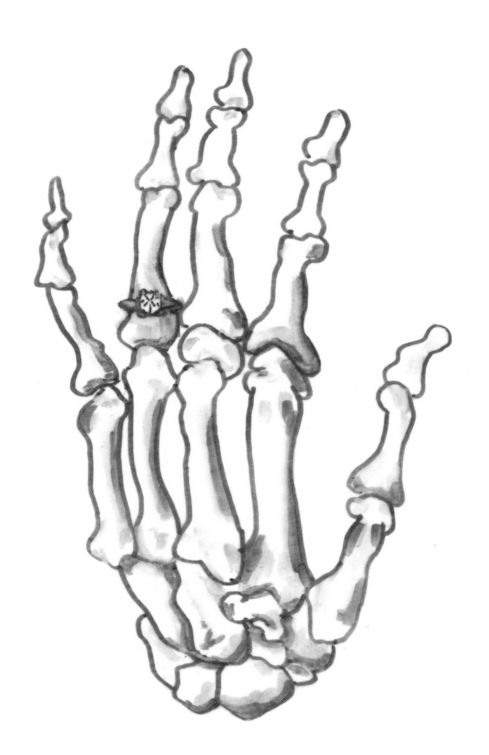

what she made of that. When coworkers ask about my girlfriend I correct them, saying that Max is trans and goes by he. Then they ask me if I've read *The Argonauts*.

It's funny the conflicting ways you can feel. I was disgusted by the thought of wanting something as banal as marriage, and yet wanted it with such intensity I made myself physically ill from crying. Eventually we married at Brooklyn City Hall. We were too unprepared to have brought a witness, but an industrious citizen offered his services, witnessing our union for a fee of fifty dollars.

Marriage and monogamy arose around the same time as agriculture, about 5,000 years ago. But romantic marriage has only been a thing for 250 years. We visited Max's parents and told them the news. We're married! Just like heterosexuals! Like us, they were unsure how to react.

Rituals are bewildering. When we first got the box with my father's ashes, Candy, Mom, and I were unsure what to do. Mom wanted to scatter them in the sea but forget it, you have to be at least three miles from shore and that was a bit too Dexter. It's illegal to sprinkle them in any public parks or on the beach. They'll probably just sit there indefinitely in the trunk of Candy's Subaru.

"Can you please drive?" Mom asks, handing me the keys. The traffic is very slow. We sit for a while without talking. Eventually, she takes a small wooden box out of her purse.

"What's that?" I ask.

"It's the rest of your father. Candy insisted on sharing him with me." She pulls a plastic bag filled with gray dust out of the box and dumps it out the window. "The box is pretty," she says, offering it to me.

One million steel caskets filled with chemically preserved bodies are buried in the U.S. each year. There are greener options though. You can have your body rolled up in an organic grass blanket and dumped into a hole to naturally decompose. You can have your ashes mixed into a fake plaster reef and launched into the ocean to become a habitat for sea life. A whole family, should they all die at once, can be made into one reef. Pets included.

Mom rubs hand sanitizer between her palms and up her forearms to the elbow. When she's finished, she checks her hair in the visor mirror. "We put a pull-out couch in Sharon's studio," she says, tucking the little box into the glove compartment.

Sharon is my mother's partner. She's older than my mother, but younger than my father was. She favors long, flowy dresses, round glasses, and tons of jewelry, like Auntie Mame if she'd had a Wiccan phase. Sharon is black and my mother is white, and they deflect the racist microaggressions constantly thrown at them by staying angry. There's no laughing anything off. Ever. As best friends they were pretty great. But as a couple they are a force.

When I was a kid, Sharon and her husband Bob were my parents' closest friends. The four of them met at a swingers' meet-up, a monthly event held in a motel near the airport. I know all about it, because my mother loves to tell the story.

When they weren't hanging out with other swingers, my folks and Sharon and Bob went to Tantric retreats and hung out at a hot spring in Mendocino that catered to the Ren Faire set. It had giant warm pools full of fat bearded guys who identified as satyrs. It was the cruiseiest place you've ever been; horny old men, menopausal witches, and non-mythological creatures too. Women like my mom, pendulous breasts tanned to a deep brown, dark nipples pointed at their bellies.

The neopagan set is overwhelmingly white, though they borrow their semiotics from cultures that are not. It's the main reason Mom and Sharon finally gave up on that scene. Well-meaning white liberals and their ankh tattoos, too dumb to know what culture they're appropriating. My friend Rachel came to the hot springs with us and an older couple trapped her in the stargazing pool, lavishing her with racist compliments. She had the body of an African Queen, they said. Rachel never went back. "These people will probably die stupid," Sharon says.

It's all gone now, anyway. Burned in the valley fire. I wasn't prepared for the pictures in the news—just a charred spot in the middle of a stretch of brown.

For years, Sharon and Bob and my parents held Sunday family dinners, a peaceful coexistence of countless backyard barbeques. Then one summer night when I was sixteen, my mother said, "Sharon and I want to tell you all something." We were all seated around the picnic table in the back yard.

She and Sharon were in love. Bob already knew. Sharon had told him privately. He'd made his peace with it. Bob was like that, easy going. Sometimes you had to check him for a pulse. He held Sharon's hand while my mom explained that she and Sharon were going to move in together. "But we don't want to break up the friendship the four of us have," Sharon added, as if my mother were just switching roommates.My father did not adjust to this news as smoothly as Bob. He set down his potato salad with disgust, like Big Daddy in *Cat on a Hot Tin Roof.* "Bullshit," he said.

"Henry, it's all been decided," my mother said. Everyone stared straight ahead. Bob patted Sharon's hand and Sharon frowned as tears dripped down my mother's face.

My parents never spoke directly to each other again. Any communication between the two of them was delivered through me. My dad claimed it was because Mom and Sharon hate men, which they do, but come on. Men can't even stand themselves these days.

"White men are watching their power fade away and they are scared because they've benefitted from their own bigotry their entire lives," says Sharon when the subject comes up, sweeping her arms like she's delivering a prophecy.

Now we're all so post. We are post marriage. We are post gay. We are post trans. We're entirely made of posts. When Max began taking testosterone, we had so much sex. I'm not supposed to notice that anything is different. But we were already having a lot of sex. We had a lot of sex plus more sex. We did it multiple times a day. It was the good kind of too much sex; not the bad kind. The bad kind is when you don't really like the person or you're always drunk or high. When you disappear except for a giant gaping hole that never seems to get filled. It's some *In the Realm of the Senses* meets Dennis Cooper feeling where you wake up the next day and parts of you are broken or there's blood and shit on the bed.

This was the great kind of too much sex. It was the kind of sex you have when you are falling in love and everything is new. Except, I was already in love with Max. I'd been in love with him for years. He was flush with androgens and bolstered by a newly discovered intrepidity, and for weeks we fucked constantly. We couldn't get enough. Once he fucked me on a flight from New York to San Francisco, right there in our seats, with people all around us. He put the tray table down and wedged his hand between my legs. I don't know if people knew what we were doing, we weren't being careful at all. We were making noise and staring at each other and acting insane. It was like being in a private bubble of sex and I didn't care what was going on around us.

I loved every new way his body would respond to mine and every new way he wanted to fuck me. I can't really let go unless I know the other person wants it. I was amazed at the things my body could do. I have loved every version of both of our bodies, and anyway, bodies are so beside the point. I loved the way he felt and looked when we were naked, but the fact that he also liked it was very sexy.

I feel defensive here. As if it's weird to desire a person you also love. Normal is just a series of actions that we've performed enough times that we've come to expect them. I explain this to my students often, and they repeat it back to me in their smart papers about pornography or the marketing of BDSM. They are so blasé. I once gave them a Gayle Rubin essay called "Temple of the Butthole." It's about the Catacombs, an underground fisting club in 1980s San Francisco. Rubin describes a wall of slings, and next to each one a large can of Crisco. Buttholes are lined up waiting to be fisted. "What else ya got?" the students asked me, bored.

They still get stuck, though, on the idea that we must have a sexual identity. Current wisdom says that each sexual act gives rise to an impenetrable identity: straight, lesbian, gay, bisexual, transgender, queer, intersex, asexual. But two million years of evidence suggest that we are capable of an eros more vast than we currently imagine. There are Paleolithic-era dildos. Neolithic Shamans experimented with herbs and the urine of pregnant animals to change their sex. The Venus of Willendorf, which your undergrad art teacher probably told you was a fertility idol, was actually pornography. There are hundreds of Venus dolls. Some are round and fleshy like the famous Willendorf Venus. Some are thin and clothed. Some wear restraints around their wrists and ankles. Some are wildly adorned. Some have penises, some have vulvas, and some have both.

Before teaching, I spent a bunch of years working in and around the porn industry. My first job entailed writing capsule descriptions of porn videos in order to make searchable online databases. I got paid per video description and quickly became insanely good at it, sometimes earning 500 bucks a day. There were lists of euphemisms and slang terms for genitals tacked to the walls; helpful when you'd written cock or pussy too many times. Watching porn for hours on end takes a toll, though. I'd get home at 2 a.m., drink a whole bottle of wine and have anxiety dreams about watching my grandmother urinate into a dog bowl.

I left that job and eventually became editor of a porn magazine. Every year I went to the AVN awards, aka, the Porn Oscars. One year I got invited to be on a panel of judges on a porn set. It was part of a gimmick that the producer had come up with to set his all-girl gang-bang porn off from all the other all-girl gang-bang porn. He told me, "The girls love doing my videos. It's like a party."

The judges, there were five of us, were supposed to watch the action while it was being taped, and vote for the girl who we thought gave the best performance. The winner got 250 bucks in cash. The producer told us to vote for "Whoever has the best orgasm," adding, "Take a point off if they fake it."

I directed lots of shoots for the magazine, and usually it was fun, or at least as much fun as watching people fuck can be—it kind of depends on who is doing the fucking. But mainstream porn is pretty tedious. One of the other judges kept talking about how much he liked to eat ass. "Really clean ass," he said. The producer pulled me aside at one point and said, "When guys say stuff like that it's because they're insecure."

We were at a giant house in the suburbs with beige carpet, beige furniture, beige everything. The performers hid in the upstairs hall while they waited for the shoot to start. None of them wanted to talk to me so I wandered around the house checking stuff out. Someone had set lunch out

for the cast. It was an open bag of Wonder Bread, a jar of Miracle Whip with a knife stuck in it, a package of bologna and couple 2-liter bottles of Diet Coke. One of the crew members saw me looking at the food and said, "Eat, baby. Go ahead."

It was ninety degrees outside. There was a pool that no one could swim in because they'd all done their makeup and hair. Before the shoot, the producer interviewed girls by the pool, asking them about their turn-ons and what they do when they aren't making porn. It was all part of this new thing where women in porn are expected to have fun and really enjoy themselves. As soon as the world discovered that women really were capable of sexual pleasure, they wanted to monetize it.

It's hard to have sex, to really get into it, without thinking about porn. It's everywhere. Max tried to make a video of us. He set his phone up on the nightstand. We were at a conference in Savannah, Georgia. The hotel was lavish. There was an enormous claw-foot tub in the middle of our room. It was like a movie set. I couldn't watch the video. I was surprised by my body. I didn't love it. My dirty talk horrified me. My vocabulary, oh god. We're both English professors; it's a problem. I think at one point I said, "Debase me." I begged him to delete it.

Bodies are terrible as often as they're fantastic. "Annie," my mother said to me the year after she dropped thirty pounds. "I'll never be able to wear a bathing suit again. I'm still a young woman. I have many, many years of life ahead of me." Her post-divorce bosom hung unceremoniously somewhere near her navel.

"Mom, you realize perky breasts are not essential to a happy life," I told her.

"Honey, you are twenty-two years old. You have no idea what's essential to a happy life." The surgeon suggested implants. From the side, my sixty-eight-year-old mother looks like an early Pam Anderson.

.

Mom and Sharon's house is bright and airy with large, south-west-facing Palladian windows that look out over the bay all the way to the city. The glass is sparkling clean. Behind the house is a detached garage that they've refinished and made into a study. Beyond the garage is a hot tub and beyond the hot tub is a canyon, too deep and overgrown to explore. Sometimes a neighbor's dog or cat will get out and become coyote food.

She brings us two glasses of pale green tea, no ice, a tiny sprig of mint on top she pinched from the herb box on the porch. She sets the glasses on two tile coasters and sighs, "Well, at least that's over."

I shrug. I stopped paying attention to my father years ago. "Your father was grotesque," she adds.

She's not wrong. Dismayed by his failing body, he was more unbearable than ever. He called the hospice nurses either faggots or cunts. No one wanted to care for him. Mom and Sharon had mostly ignored him for the past decade.

"Do you have any booze?" I ask her.

Mom knits her eyebrows, the space between them folding into two deep lines, then retrieves a mostly full bottle of bourbon from the cupboard. I pour a little into my tea and hand it back. She pours some into hers, pauses, and pours a little more. "How's Max?" Mom asks.

I tell her he's fine. And he is. "We had some therapy," I say. She looks bored. After a few minutes of sipping tea, she excuses herself to nap. Our therapist's name was Rand but sometimes we called him Brad or Dan or any one of a number of lazy homonyms. Not to his face, of course. He told us to use "I" statements to express our feelings. So Max said to me, "'I' think you're a bitch."

Marriage counseling has its roots in eugenics. It became popular in the 1930s. There was general panic that the ease with which couples could suddenly divorce would lead to a breakdown of social purity; that middle-class white couples would become a minority. The social hygiene movement began urgently promoting marriage to the middle class. By the 1960s, marriage counseling was officially a thing, though for most of the mid-century the focus was on teaching women to obey their husbands. Middle-class women fared better than their poorer counterparts though, who were unknowingly sterilized.

I leave my tea and drift toward their many books, a library amassed over years of conscientious collecting. On the shelves, there are two framed photos of me. In one, I am standing on a balcony, a large goat hair pashmina wrapped around my neck and shoulders. I'm somewhere in Nepal, and behind me you can see the Himalayan mountain range. In the other photo, I'm in their kitchen, talking on a wall-mounted phone, the long cord wrapped around my fingers. My hair is short and I am very, very tan and very thin. I vaguely remember this day, not the day exactly, but the time when it was taken and the reason I was there.

I had just come back from a long backpacking trip in Central America, and was living at their house while I figured out where to go next. I'd met up with my friend Sara, who'd broken up with her boyfriend, a sexy, macho guy who cheated on her with women they both knew. Sara had rented a small house in the jungle just off the main drag of a small town occupied mostly by backpackers, B-list rock stars, and not yet famous members of the Phoenix family. Our little house had walls on two sides and the rest was open. We slept on the second floor, our beds draped in mosquito netting.

A mango tree dangled over our front porch and capuchin monkeys the size of well-fed cats darted from limb to limb, pulling mangos off the branches and eating them. They were very territorial about the mangoes and completely unafraid of us. Instead of retreating when we walked by, they would hop to a closer branch and screech at us or climb to higher branches and rain pee down on us. Red land-crabs lived in the rainforest and crawled into the house and across our floor like cockroaches.

Cocaine was very easy to come by. Strangers would offer it to you in the discotheque the way you might offer to light someone's cigarette. People carried it in tiny plastic bags sealed with twist ties, and when you wanted some you would open the little baggie and scoop a small amount out with the end of the twist tie and sniff it.

One night, we got so high we stopped speaking English. I was surprised at how much Spanish I actually spoke. With drugs and alcohol, I was nearly fluent. We'd gotten a ride to the disco from our friend Manny. He was sweet and short and heavy-set. He wore a tank top with multiple gold chains. Sara got tired early on. "I've had enough," she leaned in close and yelled into my ear. "I'm going back to the house." But Manny grabbed my hand and said, "Stay," offering a little baggie to me. So I sat outside the disco with him as he tried to hit some kind of chemical pinnacle.

The disco was cut right into the jungle. It had a cement floor and big speakers and a grass roof, no walls. I was sweating heavily from dancing. We were yelling, even though we were sitting inches apart. He kept shoving the tiny scoop of coke under my nose, and then under his nose, and then under mine. Somehow we'd become connected, and Manny offered me the coke with the same intensity that he wanted it for himself. "I have to go home!" I yelled.

There was another guy with us, another friend of Manny's, not high, just hanging out, and he tried to intervene, tugging at Manny's arm. I was starting to worry he would want some kind of payment. He was a friend, but I'd only known him a few months, and men giving you lots of drugs rarely turns out well.

I got anxious. Manny wasn't letting me say no. Or, I was saying no but he wasn't listening. "Manny, I'm not going to have sex with you!" I yelled, even though he was right there. But it came out like Manny, blahblahblah.

He yelled back, "It's okay. It's okay." And then he shoved the little spoon under my nose again.

The friend said, "She doesn't want anymore. She's done!"

Manny said, "It's okay. It's okay."

I didn't get it. What was okay? "I don't want to have sex with you!" I yelled again.

And he repeated, "I don't want to have sex with you!"

I thought he was making fun of me. I put my hand up in the stop position like a traffic cop. "No sex!"

Manny gave me the oddest look. He cocked his head and leaned in slowly, looking at me with what I thought could be pity. Then he pointed to himself and yelled, "*Soy maricón! Soy maricón.*"

So funny that I didn't know. I didn't feel embarrassed. I felt relieved.

I told this story to Ian on one of our walks. We were in Prospect Park, sitting near the dog beach. The sun seemed enormous and close, framed by bare trees, just beginning to set. There were nests in the trees, large, formidable-looking nests like fortresses. Ian looked at the sun, then at his phone, and announced that it was 4:09 p.m.

The park was crowded that day. People streamed in from other boroughs hoping to spot the Painted Bunting, a colorful bird that had been tricked by warm weather into hanging out in Brooklyn. It was in the *Times*. This was a special bird, they said. For birders, it was like spotting a unicorn. Everyone wanted in on the action. WNYC referred to it as the Liberace of Birds, due to what they called its flamboyant coloring. The Prospect Park Alliance had trapped a feral cat in the area that they claimed was stalking the gay little bird. Poor kitty, we thought. That would have been the catch of a lifetime.

Perfect

Katie and I cleaned together.
Perfect.

The sheepshearers came today.
Perfect.

And in the morning
the milk was perfect.

A woman of the cloth.
Perfect.
Fell into her cloth.
Perfect.

The animal stink
perfects the animal.

Katie and I slept.
Perfect.
In a perfect blue dress.
I went after her hands.
Perfect.

The animated hand.

The rain gathered up.
And the path was
too perfect to stop.

I went after the cows.
Perfect.
I went after Comfort, the horse.

I fixed my love buttons.
I fixed them again.

I woke up like this.
In the hard rain.

Was getting wetter at the pump.

Katie and I fucked each other.
Perfect.
Considering all the things that bite.

I took the tucks out of my skirt.
Sounded pretty. Perfect.

Enchanted girls in a bark box.
Perfect.
Made a bonnet out of black lace.

She calls herself a huntress.

Dons male apparel
and adopts an inner life.

Terrible

I am not able.
Terrible as a truck full of chickens.
Terrible as a sun-bent ripple.
Terrible nipple.

I'm in a state.
The news is terrible.
Hardly a thought has begun
before all thoughts are terrible.

I have a terrible stain on my shirt.
This food is terrible.
Ten terrible looking dogs bound over
with their ten terrible mouths
and their hunger.

On the rocks by the river, a couple puts its arms
around each other. Terribly public
and terrible ardor. I am terribly long
like a building. I touch the terrible skyline
with my terrible sandal tan. It is terrible to see
the sun go. This is not my boat,
my sunless boat.
These are not my dogs, my black, stout dogs.
These are not my shoes, these are everyone's shoes
and the shoes of every child
in a terrible heap of trash
on a terrible island
in a terrible park
possible to enter.

You look terrible.
And your heart looks too.

And the terrible sewage treatment plant
lights up its glowing orbs. And the terrible creek
waxing noxious floats an armada.
A shimmering armada shakes sand from its sails,
every grain of it terrible as glass.

VALÉRIE MRÉJEN

from *"Eau Sauvage"*

I think I'm about to make a very serious decision because now this is getting out of hand. Starting tomorrow it's over, I don't want to hear from you again.

Something's the matter, no? You can trust me, I'd like to help you even if I'm clumsy about it. I'm often afraid to ask, I don't want to offend you. But I can tell that you're uneasy.

    You can leave the room right now, if you're just going to sit there and pout. You'd think the weight of the world was on your shoulders. I'm through with you, get out of here.

This time, I've made up my mind. I don't want to see you anymore. It's a difficult step, but I prefer this solution. Get out of my sight forever.

But my dear, you must talk, you can't always keep things buried inside. You seem sad. Maybe I'm not the most sensitive, I'm not good at putting things into words, but I'd like to help you. You can't just sit there like a stone.

I can't fall asleep until you've come home. When you live by yourself, you can stay out late, I won't even know it and I'll live in peace. But if I don't hear the key turning in the lock, I'm afraid something's happened to you, that you've been attacked in the metro, beaten up by thugs, raped, you name it.

Allô, bonjour sweetheart, everything okay? No it's just I saw in the paper this morning that a building burned down in the 11th and since you're in the 12th I thought of you and I worried it might be your place.

How are you sweetheart? You like it there? You're working hard? You're having fun, going out once in a while? Making friends? It's a positive experience, then? That's good. I'm happy to hear from you.

    How irritating you all are. I swear sometimes I want to give you a good hard smack. You sit there like a bunch of mutes. But what world do we live in? Are we strangers? We barely ever speak to each other. You might tell each other how you're doing, you might say, oh, I don't know, I had a good day or a bad day, I worked. But instead, everyone keeps quiet and looks after their own interests.

You're not old, you're not a cripple or a half-wit, you're young, beautiful, intelligent. Some people are born with a deformed hand, an ear missing, a crooked jaw, a twisted arm. Now those are real problems. You, you're not like that: you've got two ears, a mouth, a nose. You can walk on your own two feet. Some people have to get around in a wheelchair. You, thank God, you're healthy. The sun is shining, you can go out, breathe the fresh air, walk around: you should thank heaven. You're one of the lucky ones. Others don't have the choice, they're handicapped, they have a disease. You've got a good head on your shoulders, you're smart, well-adjusted. That's the main thing. Some people are born crosseyed, with a shrunken brain, a screw loose. You, you're not a freak. You're well brought up, polite. You can't let yourself be tormented. I know you've got your troubles but believe me, it's not worth it.

You're not an idiot, you're not a cow. You're healthy, beautiful, young. Why sit there moping? It'd be one thing if you were, I don't know, a hunchback. But you have everything. You can't let yourself get so low. Plenty of people have good reason to feel miserable. But you, you've got brains, a body. What more can you ask for? How can you possibly be sad? You should be out singing in the street.

Sure, I grant you, anyone can feel worried or depressed sometimes. But if you look objectively at the situation, you have no reason to be anxious. Do you even realize? You could have been born an imbecile. But instead, you're normal. And on top of that, you have good qualities.

I'm telling you, my dear, you mustn't give up hope. You have worries? Then talk about them. It's not shameful. Everybody has worries. You can tell me these things. I don't always have the answers, but I have experience. I can help you. It's my duty.

People who are lame, bedridden, who have genetic diseases, those are real problems.

Well, I'm just about to lose it. You come here, you sit around feeling sorry for yourself . . . It makes me sick. I've got enough on my mind without having to deal with your little tantrums. I come home tired and I see you sulking. You think that's nice? I'd like a little warmth around here, some laughter. But no, you're mute as a fish. Do me a favor, get out of the living room. And if you keep it up I'll have to make a serious decision, it's insufferable.

From time to time you could say, "I'm going to make a salad." And like that, you'd make something to eat. Something easy, pasta or an omelet, whatever you want.

You'd cook a little dinner, whatever you like, it's all the same to me as long as it's your idea.

You'd take that initiative. It would come naturally to you. One evening, you'd open the refrigerator and you'd throw together a meal.

I want some affection. For you to ask me if I've had a good day. For you to be helpful, considerate, kind.

For you to have more than two words to say. When you go out with friends you all talk amongst yourselves, so why isn't it the same with me? I'd give anything to know what you've been learning, what you're doing, if you've had a good afternoon.

I don't know who your friends are, where you go at night.

He's at university, then?

What's his religion?

His parents live where?

And what do they do?

How did you meet?

These friends of yours, I'm not saying there's anything wrong with them. But you should also spend time in bourgeois circles, see other sorts of people. If you want to come with me one day, I can bring you along. I have some wonderful friends with children your age. No, you don't have to; but you should give it a chance, listen, observe and form your own opinion. Either you'll meet someone, or you'll say to yourself this isn't for me, but at least you'll know that you tried.

They have a daughter, I adore her, she's such a modest girl, and shy

. . . I'd like you to get to know her. Come at least once. Little by little, you'll start fall in with a circle of friends, a group you can join to go out dancing, or to restaurants, to go running in the park.

You've got to come once and judge for yourself. I'd like for you to talk with their son. Maybe you'll like him or maybe you'll think he's a moron. But if you think he's nice, all the better, you'll have an interesting conversation and he'll introduce you to his friends. That's how you establish relationships. You'll go once, twice, and after a while you'll start to grow on people and they'll invite you to things.

Last night I went to see some friends of mine who have a brilliant son.

You should tidy yourself up a little. It's a shame, you're not bad looking and you cover yourself up with these bed-sheets. Anyone would take you for an Arab. You could wear a skirt every so often, stockings, a blouse, heels, a brooch, a bracelet. You're completely hidden under that *gandoura*. I mean, sure, it's the fashion, but there are limits.

Listen, honestly. What are these dresses that come down to your ankles? Are you trying to punish yourself? Why these clothes, when a tailored suit would look so nice on you? Go buy yourself one: here, I'm giving you money! I don't understand why you hide under that thing. It's a spacesuit!
    Really, it's as if you're dressed to go to the moon. You'd look so much nicer in black tights, with a little jacket . . . Come with me one day, we'll go to a boutique and I'll buy you an outfit.

My friends' daughter, she's so sweet. And elegant. She always has impeccable clothes.
    They have beautiful children, well brought-up, when you walk in the door they run to hug you and throw their arms around your neck.

Allô, bonjour sweetheart, are you doing well? I called you yesterday, but there was no answer. Ah, you were out.

Allô, I'm trying to call your landline, but I keep getting a busy signal. Ah, you're on the phone. Well, call me when you're done.

Bonjour sweetheart, I'm calling you from the hiking trail, we're in the woods outside of Paris, it's very cold and rainy, lots of wind, listen if you have a minute tomorrow call me, I'll be happy to hear from you. I hope you're doing well and you had a good day.

Bonjour darling, well, haven't heard from you for two days. I'm sure you're doing fine. Call me when you have a chance. Love you.

I tried to reach you several times, I don't know what's going on with you, give me a call one of these days so I can relax a little. It's been at least two weeks since I heard your voice. Me, I've got a lot on my mind and a fever, but anyway I'm okay, it's not serious. Well, love you, goodbye.

I can't stand New Year's parties, I prefer to spend the evening at home. If it's just to go out in the street and find myself in the middle of a screaming crowd . . . No, I bought myself a little salmon and I watched TV. Oh, well, you know, the usual garbage . . . *2 Hours to Seduce* and pfffft, really mindless stuff, I watched for a while and then I went to bed.

Translated by Katie Shireen Assef.

JENNIFER ADAMS

Girl on a Balcony

Bell invited me out to dinner tonight. Bell doesn't drink. He's a scholar. He translates *Tristan and Iseult* from the French. We're drinking ice water and we're talking about his ex Paul and my ex Eric. Six months ago, we were all friends. We were in the same restaurant as now, eating tapas and drinking wine, laughing about love.

But now it's just Bell and me, talking about the men who are missing, the men who are children.

I say, At least your child didn't try to kill you.

Paul cheated on Bell with strangers. Bell's going to the clinic tomorrow morning, to take another test.

I tell Bell I'm learning to knit in my convalescence, and Bell says, I'd like to knit that boy a condom.

Bell is from South Texas.

Bell says, At least your child didn't put his penis on Craigslist.

That's the joke of the week. The title of Paul's ad is "It's Practically Winter Already." Paul wears a gray athletic T-shirt to cover his belly, and below, an erection. It's a veiny, not-that-impressive unicorn horn, stabbed into an ungroomed Black Forest of pubes. Behind that, in the blue screen glow, is Paul's apartment wall, covered in Paul's poems.

I remind Bell that Paul posted the ad in early October, the day he visited me in the hospital. Bell says, He can't even tell the truth about the seasons.

I ask the waiter, Did you know that it's practically winter already?

It makes Bell laugh.

Now it really *is* practically winter already.

Bell is dating an emergency room doctor, and tells me about the doctor over a dish of olives. I tell him that Paul called me at two a.m. this morning. Paul keeps calling me but I don't answer. Paul is the kind of person who yells over you on the phone, the kind who has to one-up your stories. Bell calls him Meatball, because we were talking about big meatballs once, and Paul said how he ate the biggest meatball anyone could ever have eaten.

Bell and I are listeners. We just listen. We listen, and then we give. We give you a leg and a foot if you ask. We throw in an eye—the good one.

I say, I edited Eric's work for him. I made macaroni and cheese from a children's cookbook and held him when he was curled in a ball, crying about how terrible a writer he was. I told him how special he was.

Special indeed, Bell says.

The cheese plate comes and Bell says about Paul, That boy didn't know anything about gourmet food before me. *Please.* He bought lunch meat in a plastic container from CVS before I showed him better. He'd never eaten prosciutto. He thought Velveeta was macaroni and cheese.

Paul keeps calling because he thinks I'm the road back to Bell, but Bell assures me that that road is permanently closed. A couple of weeks back, Paul was going on about wanting to die. I listened. I thought, *You* did this... *You* left Bell. This was *your* choice. An hour later Paul texted me and said he had gone to the store and was about to make meatloaf for himself. I called him and said suicidal people don't make meatloaf.

I tell Bell, Do you know I took sleeping pills when I took Eric back in June? I went to the doctor after Eric ran away, and they gave me a prescription for sleeping pills. "Whenever things get heated," the doctor said, "take a pill." So I bought a pill cutter and walked around with halves and quarters. I'd take three quarters when things got heated. There was a lot of sex. And TV. We watched this one show. A woman got pregnant and her boyfriend left her. He said he couldn't handle the pressure. She came home one day to find him packing his bags. She confronted him and there was a huge ugly fight. She said all manner of true and hateful things. All the things I wanted to say myself.

I stop talking and look at the fancy cheese in front of Bell and me, a few pallid slivers dressed up with honey and jam. She had a lot of courage, I say. Television courage. Eric said, I wouldn't have left you. I would have been there. And I said, but you *did* leave. I said, You *weren't* there.

The waiter brings a casserole of beets, and Bell says, The hearts of Eric and Paul, roasted.

I say, No those are *ours.*

Not mine, honey. My heart is made of stone.

Bell's ex before Paul died. He was a drug addict, and broke up with Bell after a relapse. Bell got a call a few months later from his ex's sister. Bell's ex had died in the bathroom, drowned. A few dealers had come over and found him passed out, picked through his things, and left.

Bell keeps his dead ex's shirts in their own drawer. He sealed them all in Ziplocs, and double-bagged the one his ex was wearing the day they met. This was an issue for Paul. Paul didn't understand the Shirt-in-a-Baggie, as he called it. But bottom line, I don't think Bell's heart is made of stone.

Eric couldn't stay away, I say to Bell. He'd call me, or wait outside the building and talk his way back into the apartment, and then he'd scream at me as soon as he'd get in the door. He'd talk as if we were still together, yelling about old things, pacing the rooms. I'd say, It's over, Eric. He'd say, I love you. I don't know what to do with it. He'd say, I'm not happy. I'm not mentally well. I'd say, I know that, Eric; that's clear to me. He'd say, I can't be in a relationship, but I love you. I say to Bell, What does that mean? Tell me, what kind of bullshit is that?

That's big bullshit. That's what it is.

The thing is, I say to Bell, I felt bad for him. So bad, he'd stay the night. I drove him home one morning and we talked Heidegger in the car, because he and Eric were both Nazis, and then he kissed me and pushed a bottle full of Xanax with someone else's name on it into my palm. *These will relax you*, he said. What kind of boyfriend doles out pills, someone else's pills?

When you showed me that bottle, Bell says, I told you to throw it out.

Bell's heard the story before, but I still can't believe it myself, so I keep telling it. I say, Are you kidding? I kept it to show the police. And a week later, there Eric was, asking me about "the status of the supply." I only entertained his advances because of what your child Meatball said—you know, I wish you guys could find a way to be together, you were such a good couple. Meatball couldn't stand change, even if it meant developing an addiction to a federally controlled substance.

Nostalgia, Bell says. Paul was nostalgic.

Yes, I say. Nostalgia will get you every time. You wake up and drive around the city all day, looking for ghosts. Your home is gone, and you go looking for it, not realizing the Zoning Committee of Heartbreak has razed your building.

The Freight Train of Pain took a diversion through your backyard.

You turn to say something—you want to say something, the littlest of things, stupid things like, did you know that Napoleon drank cologne? A blue moon is the second full moon of a calendar month? A woman's heart beats faster than a man's? The average person laughs fifteen times a day? You turn to say something, and you're talking to lint and an unbuckled seatbelt. You're conversing with The Void.

My relationship with Paul *was* The Void, *and* it was devoid of humor. I think I laughed fifteen times all of last year.

    Paul certainly laughed.

    At my expense, yes.

Bell walks me home in the dark. He's a walker-home of newly single women. He recites *Tristan and Iseult* along the way. He says, *We greet those who are cast down, and those in heart, and those troubled, and those filled with desire.*

    Tonight he adds the "we." Tonight, he quotes by heart.

    We are all troubled, I say, kicking stones along the pavement.

    We are all filled with desire, Bell replies.

    I don't say this to Bell, but I think my heart is beating faster than his. I think about happiness, and if it exists or not, or if it will ever happen again, or if it's more of an event than an abstraction. A happening, like Halley's comet.

    It seems like happiness does exist, but as a momentary and plural thing. You know, as a kitchen and a pair of human beings. A couple washing dishes, making it through the day to evening. The scenario can get more elaborate if you like. Maybe the radio is on, and the man sings opera poorly but with exuberance. Maybe the people hold each other against the warmth of the electric stove, the sink running hot, the lights switched on and bright. Maybe they think, We are fed and the bills are paid and we laugh together. We are blind to the future, but together we try to hold off the coming of the darkness.

We stand outside my building and I tell Bell that Eric used to catch me off guard in the kitchen. I'd scream and he'd catch me in his arms till I couldn't get away.

    It was the right kind of scream, I say. It was the right kind of not being able to get away. That's happiness, right? When, for a second, you think you're going to die together?

    Maybe, Bell says.

    We hug and say goodnight. I can tell that Bell is nervous.

    I say I might text Meatball later, to make sure he's okay. I say, My heart is made of plaster of Paris.

I'm on my balcony standing in the cold. When Eric moved out, he moved a block away. I can see his bedroom window from here. If he can see me, I imagine I'm the size of a lit matchstick. I imagine the electric deck lights make me burn in the dark. Bell says to put a screen up. That, or a large and handsome male mannequin.

Between us lie tarpaper roofs and bare trees, a road full of cars, two parallel sidewalks traced with the life of strangers. The night is quiet.

Since Eric is gone, it's just getting through the day. It's waking up. It's moving a body that feels like someone else's to the shower. Brushing your teeth, combing your hair, trying to eat something.

Some days there are moments of reprieve. You forget for a second where you are or who you are, and how you got there, and there are some nights without dreams.

Most nights he comes to me in dreams and we talk. We sit and we talk.

The other night he came and sat on our bed, on our old quilt, and he said to me, It's time. I had no idea what he was talking about. But he was so calm that I replied like I knew.

I said, I know. I said, I don't want much. I don't need much.

He said, I know you don't.

And that was that. I should have said, Yeah, I guess that's why you treated me so badly.

I should have said a lot of things.

They tell you it hurts less and less with time.

But some days it hurts more, no matter how many weeks pass, or what anyone says about the one you've lost, or how much you know about the universe, or how many times you laugh in twenty-four hours.

Some days you feel like the honeysuckle pulled from Iseult's hazelnut tree.

Hey, you say to the sea between your buildings. *Hey, give me my nut tree back.*

HANNAH BROOKS-MOTL

Stanford

Come out of your program, we're all poolside.
The mirror is majestic and raw and just

like biology. Come honor the particularized
salon, its endurance of the jailor.

The judge. And the amputee.
What is the true relation between numbers

and tears? Apocryphally, the woman
called it off we think with her sadness.

It was more self-management by seminar, by
trial. On fringes. Full of asymptotes

and glamorous phrasing, and inclusive
of singular emotions here on our quad

where I'm watching the sources
of funding. In pursuit of pastoral energies

and convincing friendship, I have come
to care for the display and our sense

of being underwritten. Everyone
must ache, to be so underwritten

in the furthered operations
of the real.

EDWIN TORRES

Lucifer's G-Spot

In psuedo light baked for lovely lies
the heaving dirt seems fresher
when the back is turned
to really talk about grabbing ass
out of context try leaving a tip
bigger than the prize here we go
the table set low to waist
the moment of facing up is when
the costume is revealed competition
means who has the fastest come job
don't you play those games like
sex olympics where you try to make
the other come first I always win or
try to you she asks green eyes concealing
a curve behind vanity the perfect bottom
is one that leaves room for improvement
mine a few inches at a time if three minutes
were a bomb I'd be Lucifer with a sundial
what is it I'm looking for in an empty room
for a rise to happen without encouragement
without expectation the doctor plays the infidel
suggesting two glasses of water where one
would kill look he says you have no trouble
with solids just let the daily whizz replay
letting my hands loose is what started this
what would you do to me she says bend
me over and I tune in to a debate between
time zone and equanimity did I have your
fee wrong is that why you think I was so
generous the light dimmed below a whisper
still no luck with a stroke when it won't
win I hate to lose she says immediately turning
rear to front in the hopes of some sort of

jobless surrender take it she seems to say
take what you see as a way to complete your
goals even if they don't jive with mine but skin
on skin has always left a scar even without a lick
having tea with you when I thought you ordered
coffee that wasn't a strong enough ending
even happy do you want one now we all know
where this come from and where this
wants some or none now the invention
of tongue over talk seems efficiently foregone
let the time on this session run out so we
can both get back to small talk centered
on soul talk sinned by the realm rimmed
in thickest observation I get no complaints
she hears holding south what sweet does
to sweat tell me something soft ok where you
close by climbing onto the table

JULIA TILLINGHAST

Sufficiency

I saw my father
I wanted him to take me home
I dropped my groceries
Into the parking lot
The parking lot
Was inky with rain
My inner music told me
To repeat myself
To hold on to the railing
To call his name
Until he wouldn't come
& instead something
More self-sufficient would happen
The parking lot was ink
I dropped my groceries
My father came
But he did not know me
Every day
I wake as a child, the sky pushing me
Into the suit of an adult
Like a child pushing
Another child's face down into water
That happened to me a lot you know
When I was a child
Another child wanting
To play at drowning me
It's interesting now
Sometimes now when I think about
Being taken, I imagine being pushed
From the back of my skull
Into a bed
Where my mouth can feel
What it means universe where speech loses

What I never could do
I am now doing
What I never wanted
I now want

Adrian C. Louis

I dreamed I was having
Sex with two dead girls
So I did what you do if can do
And went back to sleep
Sometimes the sea
Is very shallow
And the bottom of it
Is very close to your boat
And you're not so much
Floating as just
Trying not to drag
This house
Is for everything
Not just
Unrequited love
But the wrestling with the dragons of
History identity socialization
If I have paper
I can fill with black letters
I am going on record
To affirm that things are wrong
And that it can't just be
About taking sides, about violence
This house is also
About violence
I wake up reading
Your Christmas poem
Standing behind two racist soldiers at Wal-Mart
And following them out into the snow
And cursing Christ

For wrapping your fists
In the Santa Claus cloth
Of Christmas
I dreamed I was having
Sex with two dead girls
I tried to say the right thing
But what came out of my mouth
Was not words it was
Just small wrestlers
& I blushed the small blush
Of the white man who is
The alpha and omega
Of all the food I eat

Inspired by Adrian C. Louis's poem, "Christmas Carol for the Severed Head of Mangas Coloradas."

Gardening

I wonder
About the metaphysics
Of privilege if you can
Split an atom without
The apocalypse breaking
Into you if you turn
Half of it in Houston
A part of it in Providence
Will also rotate, so
What does that mean
For the deprivations
My elevation
Makes possible?
History
Is not like
Snow,
Or is it?
Increasingly
I mention snow
As a poltergeist
As a memory
As winter
Tesseracts out of
The state that I live in
A baby underneath
The marbled climate
In awe of the clouds
And I use language
To undo language
Imagining I am new here

Imagining I am feeling this
Softness for the very first time
The shadows like to
Feed their faces
On berries and sweet lettuce
When do penises become whips become
Aqueducts become the plumbing of throats
Become not just male, become
Pipelines become long-stemmed roses
Become Eve's
Become prayers
Become hopeful

NOY HOLLAND

Bitty Cessna

Bluebird day, a fine day to fly. They taxi out, no radio, roiling dust, the airport bleak and uncontrolled. A vulture stands on the head of a cactus and displays its wings to dry. "What's *he* waiting for?" the instructor jokes. Of course he's flirting. Horny, disappointed man, too tall to fly the fighters and color blind besides. He calls her Sunshine. A face like sunshine. First the climb, full on, the big blue he can't see. She's to stall, spin, recover. Pretty, a lay, college girl. She lives behind the hangars in a school bus. She turns the plane upside down. Everything in the cockpit is a missile now, launched, flying at their heads. Wallowing, sloppy, sickening plunge—the altimeter sweep, the stick clutched in her hands. "IT'S MY PLANE," he shouts, meaning, *let go, fool*. That we may live. May we seem to have lived. He sees again the spines of the cactus, the meaty face of the vulture, ravenous, a dream. Bitty Cessna, yellow as the dress his mother wore. Mother war. Mary. Gone to God. Mine.

Ringneck

He shot pheasant with his comrade from kindergarten, flushed from the grassy swale. The men carried the birds out on their backs. They crossed the stream, the water cold, and pain flared in his toe. The gout years. Years of good bourbon beside a fire. Like a beacon, such pain, a knuckle pulsing in the night. They cut the trip short.

Took the toe, the doctors, when at last he was home, a bright nub on the heap to be burned. Brother at last to the black man. Foreskin of an infant; polyp; liver; lung—the array of what people live missing.

First the small knuckle, next the big. Next the foot—half the foot, next the whole foot, as in the song of a boa constrictor.

It hurt him, all, even missing.

Next the leg. To bear the pain in the leg he was missing, he rubbed the leg he had left in the mirror. Which helped. Some. Still he bellowed. Raged. Threw shoes at his wife.

He arranged to have lilies delivered to his wife on their anniversary for the next twenty years.

His wife was Pretty Shield—his pet name for her. Puddy Tat. At last: Doll.

The man's name was Wing.

Wing what? Wing what?

I have loved you for years, Wing Pepper, your hands like a girl's, your mouth.

King for a Day

Ants steal other ants' babies and make them into slaves. A fact. She cannot remember much more about it. She remembers Morocco, a man whose hand was hacked off at the wrist. He had been a stupendous musician. He was drawn into a trance at a drumming ceremony and lay down, coming home, in a heap of ants. Hours later, his brother found him. He had been eaten raw. Like meat, the brother told her. He lived another three days. A killer, the brother, the other a thief. The girl was nothing. His heart kept missing. His missing hand shook. But he was king for a day on the day he died and the ants in their perfect armor bore him in glory away. Singing. Song of feasting. Song of love.

HAZEL WHITE

from "Vigilance Is No Orchard"

Motions in a body schema may begin to bunch—as textures in the garden
pick up here and here into a congregation listing toward the light—locking
with the view.

A daydream of speech becomes a form of movement, eager in the flat pride
of riding out and over, even painfully, in the sunshine.

The twist begins far

below at my feet. A body pursuing a claim
churns a frenzy of orientation.

Allows a mute part to bruise, swell, bush sideways
on the land shelf, and reset itself into survival under way.

I say right now I want to wear a man's shirt and Paul Smith summer boots—no laces, but a full enclosure. (A vow against tiptoeing and landscape as a profile of thinking.)

Here I am, the architecture close-in, the Valentine entrance, and I will raid it:

"Do I want tall or do I want ——?"

—Greene silences the architect's white wall by planting two eucalyptus trees to whistle over it. The eye hops right up, ears listen branch to moving branch, and the present tense warms what's freshly bare, revealing a woman to herself.

"Space exactly the way I want it."

"everyone is Noah" .03

hear wind cipher hear mocking   bird cipher off a bit more
morning from your untested   destiny say you see crows
as the deacons of daylight's   ministry to place them in

the fetish context breeding   as talisman a new bridge
we drove across last night so   white but the bolts won't hold up
in the next quake you expect   a court will return soon their

required conviction and   sentence you for failure of
the inspiration we call   nature printed in cursive
divined from unseen roots which   are themselves operations

of a signature you can't
pronounce but is everything's
name

For Andrew Joron.

"everyone is Noah" .04

your latest cure for landscape   the selective construction
of its object still only   exaggerates your use of
possessive pronouns your friend   wears her dog's collar as

if "theater can serve a   revisionary purpose"
says Buell but distance is so   parental generates myths
that penetrate your trinket   embedded monuments scotch

tape yellows more edges lift   can't hold anything for long
your task list scrapes off only   the first coating of what to
do next life a transparent   compression left the water

on too long again rules the   book of Genesis opens
with spirit talking the day   ends with the ritualized
death called sleep off a layer   in your production of false

charms can't tell if they're weeds or   wild medicinals large crow
eyeing you from the fence plus   a worm dry on the sidewalk
are two more doors you are ill-   equipped to access this year

if the wasp queen builds her nest
above every exit let
her

DANIEL BORZUTZKY

Lake Michigan, Scene 15

They beat me even though I did nothing

I don't know what day it was

But they beat me on the beach

They beat me with iron paws

The mayor ordered the police superintendent to beat me

The police superintendent ordered an officer to beat me

The officer ordered his dogs to attack me

Then someone beat me with iron paws

Then someone kicked me with iron boots

Then someone shot me

Then someone buried me in the sand

Then someone scooped me out of the sand and dumped me somewhere

And I was dead

But I could feel the sand on my body

I could feel the sand filling my mouth

I could feel the sand in my eyes

There was an earthquake in my eyes

There was a tornado in my mouth

But after the storms passed it was peaceful and I was dead

And they beat me even though I did nothing

They said I was illegal

They said I was an immigrant

They said I was an illegal immigrant who roamed the streets in a gang

They said I raped people

They said I killed people

They said I smuggled drugs in my gastrointestinal tract

They said I didn't speak the right language

They said my boss exploited me and I tried to kill him

They said my boss treated me well and I tried to kill him

They said my heart was dark

They said I peddled in blood

They said this was only war and that I had the audacity to think my body could resist the state

Let death come quickly   I asked

Let death be easy

But I did not know how long it would take

I did not know I would be under the sand forever

I did not know that in Chicago the bodies do not die when they have been strangled or riddled with bullets

A journalist asked the mayor why they killed us

I am not responsible   said the mayor

There will be an inquest   said the mayor

We will bring the perpetrators to justice   said the mayor

He was wearing a slim-fitting suit and he looked handsome as the hurricane entered his mouth

He was wearing a slim-fitting suit and he looked handsome as he pretended he did not live in a city of cadavers and rotten carcasses

He had gel in his hair and his shoes were nicely polished and he said there will be an inquest when what he meant was that there will be an inquisition

I died and I died again and a voice said something about hope

And another voice said you pay a big price for hope

And I dragged myself around the sand and I tried to make it to the water because I thought the water might carry me away but each time I took a step closer to the water the water moved further from my body and there were faces in the water and they were calling to me and I was trying to get to the water

It's what you do when you are dead

But every time I took a step towards the water the water drew further away

And the faces in the water were murmuring and their murmurs grew
louder and louder as I moved nearer and further

And it was only war   a voice said   by way of explanation   as he
photographed my dead body on the sand
And I was dead though I was still breathing when I finally made it to the
water

And in the water there was another war going on in the waves

And it was only the beginning of the war that would kill me again and again

Lake Michigan, Scene 16

They put paint on my eyes

They put mud on my eyes

They put sludge on my eyes

They asked me to look in a mirror

They said this is your face

They said you have been dead now for three days

They said you have been missing now for three days

They asked me what I did with my mind

They asked me what I did with my papers

They asked me when I last saw my parents

They asked me what I did with my bank card

They asked me what I did with my hands

I told them my hands were broken

I told them I didn't remember my bank card

I told them about an investigator who came to my office

He worked for the city and his title was Investigator #41

He asked me what I did on the internet
He measured my arms

He measured my legs

He asked me who I spoke to on my cell phone

He asked me who I sent messages to

He asked me if my documents had been filed according to regulation and policy

He looked inside my mouth with a flash-light

He tested my reflexes

He asked me to stand still   perfectly still   and to keep my balance

I could not keep my balance and he told me he expected me to do better

He asked me why I couldn't keep my balance

He hit me when I tried to keep my balance

He spat on me when I fell to the floor

He kicked me when I fell to the floor

He asked me to stand up   to stand perfectly still   and to try to keep my balance

He punched me in the stomach and I fell on the floor and the other workers in the office heard me scream but they could not help me and they were also beaten

He told me I helped an illegal human being and that this made me illegal

He told me I helped an illegal human being find food and as a result I would not be able to eat

He told me I helped an illegal human being drink water and as a result I would not be able to drink water

We got into a van and he took me to the prison on the shores of Lake Michigan and we went into an office and he asked me to sign some papers

I signed nothing and they beat me and locked me in a closet

He took my shirt and pants and locked the door

I sat on the cold ground

I fell asleep

Maybe I died

I woke up and there was a pipe lying next to me

I woke up and there was blood coming out of my mouth

I woke up and I was dead and there was a mountain in the middle of the beach and they took me there

I woke up and I was dead and they left me at the foot of the mountain

I saw a picture of the city in a mirror

I saw giant birds committing suicide

I saw a species of children struck with a terrible plague

They could not walk or talk

They crawled and moaned

I asked for some money and they gave me a map

I asked for some water and they gave me a few coins

I asked for my family and they showed me a picture of the mayor

I asked for an attorney and they beat me

I crawled up the mountain and it started to burn

I walked into the flames and I woke up and someone played notes from a
ram's horn

I walked out of the flames and fell asleep and I heard my mother's voice

They poured gasoline on me and I recited some numbers in my head

I tasted salt in my mouth

I tasted gasoline in my mouth

I heard the children of Chicago crying and they were buried under the
mountain

I heard the mayor say that our city was a place of sanctuary

I heard the mayor say that our city was a shelter for refugees

I saw the police shoot an innocent boy 22 times and I heard the mayor make
a promise

Your body will return   he said

Your body will be a dream that spreads slowly across the beach   he said

Your body will be a playground and the children will crawl all over you

I felt my hands burn

I felt my neck burn

I felt my fingers burn

I felt my lips burn

I felt my lungs burn

I felt my elbows burn

I felt my nose burn

My hair was burning and I asked if I could see my sister

They asked me what she looked like and I described her perfectly and they said nothing

I heard them drill into the mountain and it felt like they were drilling into my body

They drilled a hole in the mountain and the children crawled into it and sang a song to the city about how much they loved it

And the song grew softer and softer and the children sang it forever

And it is only war   said a body in uniform

It is only the beginning of war

KELLI ANNE NOFTLE

The Hair

Dude can America be
saved. My cousin has dark
almost black hair. I saw her
yesterday praying for help.
Metal new wave hair you know
the guy who looks like Elvis
and plays bass infiltrating
every sector. Well, I claim
his shed blood.
Oh God.

I need your help.
I've got to put on peroxide
I've got to have thousands
who get it on and
I've got to get these
red highlights eternalized.

Surely you can afford $20 a month
for the next ten months and
get me a crowd at Goodwill
on Saturday with J
to buy that Budweiser tee-shirt
(thousand gallon member club)
with the plaid wool pants.

The truth is I left
all my stuff in J's car
and I've got to raise
this money now.
Right now.

I need the flesh and blood
of young people
who are turned on—
eyebrow rings (nipples too).

Man give me the grace and
give me your Ramones cd.
Go to your phone right now
and I'll pay for your hair.

ALIX ANNE SHAW

Weapons Of

hallousa invitation
passeled in shampoo

lungwise ides of
eyeless shred

pathway toward an–
otherwise

body dinged with now

cogently embittered
pfistering

her whiskey on the rocks
trying to lament it

the sandscape ending
in a zeroed flat

10,000 steps an office
disposable plateau

a signed to
hella buttered sun

a syncope
synecdoche

    was, like

a bushel full of virgins
smooth as flightless

milch
arrow over arrow

litigious memory

the concrete post-it

skystained road

the night is later chilly
in winsome rain she am

on the far side   of the Chunnel
like I is   operation

Charcuterie for Suidae
pummeled   in the smoker

black salt campesino
& more &   more &   more

mon oeil gauche pleure non stop
"cold" needle, tear duct, drops etc

who knows what will feather out
pass the radial

arm

JASON MITCHELL

good sign

I found two aubergine
Amethysts tucked inside a crushed

.

Velvet pouch on one of the trails while
Hiking in the rain, and took it as a
Love charm and good sign, and the one

.

Tinier stone almost jumped out of my
Hand when I first took it out I
Bobbled it a few times before securing it

.

In the palm of my hand, and read into
The event as the small stone being you
And took that as a good sign too.

FLORENCE KINDEL

Late Afternoon

Abstinence from mask making continues
Don't turn back just yet
I flung my scissors over the pole lamp
Playing with reversible shadows
That stuck to me
Rubber cement problems must be solved
Later looking at the evening sun
A god peeked out from behind it
It was the littlest thing
And soon a second little one
Sat at my kitchen table smiling

READING LIST

GINA ABELKOP: I'm currently reading Gabrielle Civil's *Swallow the Fish* and it's excellent. Also recently read and adored: Tim Jones Yelvington's *This is a Dance Movie!*, Ariel Goldberg's *The Estrangement Principle*, Pauline Hopkins' Of One Blood. Alexander Chee's *Queen of the Night* is like that dreamed-of dessert-that-nourishes and I recommend it to everyone.

JENNIFER ADAMS: Summer reading—*The New Oxford Shakespeare: The Complete Works*, edited by Gary Taylor et al. Mary Beard's *SPQR*. Elsa Morante's *History: A Novel. Rome Stories*, edited by Jonathan Keates. Stefan Zweig's *The Post-Office Girl*. Tove Jansson's *The Summer Book*. Barbara Comyns's *The Vet's Daughter*. Margaret Atwood's *Hagseed*. Mavis Gallant's *Paris Stories* and *A Fairly Good Time*. Jane Gardam's *Old Filth Trilogy*. Martha Nussbaum's *Anger and Forgiveness*. Akhil Sharma's *A Life of Adventure and Delight*.

KATIE SHIREEN ASSEF lives in Los Angeles. Of late, she has been reading Jane Unrue's *Love Hotel*, Can Xue's *The Last Lover* (trans. Annalise Finegan Wasmoen), and Fanny Howe's *Radical Love: 5 Novels*.

OSAMA ALOMAR was born in Damascus. He is currently an Exiled Writer-in-Residence at City of Asylum in Pittsburgh. He is the author of *Fullblood Arabian* (translated from the Arabic by C.J. Collins) and *The Teeth of the Comb & Other Stories* (translated from the Arabic by the author and C.J. Collins), both published by New Directions. He is also the author of three collections of short stories and a volume of poetry in Arabic. He is currently reading Hemingway's *The Old Man and the Sea* and Gibran's *The Prophet*.

DANIEL BORZUTZKY is currently reading Roberto Bolaño's *The Third Reich* (translated by Natasha Wimmer) and *No Dictionary of a Living Tongue* by Duriel Harris.

HANNAH BROOKS-MOTL: 'Stanford' came out of reading around in midcentury social psychology, including the work of Stanley Milgram and Philip Zimbardo, and thinking about connections between experimental theater, social experiments, and institutionality. Julian Beck and Judith Malina, Michael Kirby, Anna McCarthy, Ian Nicholson, and Antonin Artaud are presences. I recommend each. Currently I'm reading and enjoying the work of Sylvia Townsend Warner, Gertrude Stein's *Wars I Have Seen*, and *Aerodrome* by Rex Warner.

LUCY BURNS: I'm currently enjoying *The Argonauts* by Maggie Nelson, *Sarah—of Fragments and Lines* by Julie Carr, *Salvage the Bones* by Jesmyn Ward, *Leaving Atocha Station* by Ben Lerner, and *Hi-Fructose Magazine*. Next on my list are *[insert] Boy* by Danez Smith and *Look* by Solmaz Sharif.

DIANA CAGE: Barbara Browning's *The Gift* is great, I'm reading it right now. I've also been carrying around *Ava* by Carole Maso, reading it in bits and pieces when I'm on the subway. There are a few books I turn to whenever I need inspiration, Dodie Bellamy's *When the Sick Rule the World* and Selah Saterstrom's *The Meat and Spirit Plan*. Oh and Sam Ace's *Home in Three Days Don't Wash*, which is getting a rerelease from Belladonna in 2018, so I've been reading it while the manuscript is getting retyped. It's so hot and dirty, everyone should read it.

MARTY CAIN: has been simultaneously reading *Frankenstein* and María Negroni's essays in *Dark Museum* (trans. Michelle Gil-Montero, Action Books, 2015). A highly compatible pairing! Lately, he's also been reading Cody-Rose Clevidence's *Beast Feast* (Ahsahta, 2014) and Valeria Mejer Caso's *This Blue Novel* (trans. Michelle Gil-Montero, Action Books, 2015).

MARI CHRISTMAS studies and writes from upstate New York. Currently pining for Alexandra Kleeman's forthcoming collection, *Imitations*, and Jen George's *The Babysitter at Rest* (in the mail!). Always, Fleur Jaggey's *Sweet Days of Discipline* and Grace Paley's *The Little Disturbances of Man*.

ELIZABETH CLARK WESSEL: Lately I've been reading Diane di Prima's *Revolutionary Letters* and the news.

AARON COLEMAN keeps getting worked up and reading poems from Eduardo C. Corral's *Slow Lightning*, Rilke's *Duino Elegies* (translated by Gary Miranda), and Ross Gay's *Catalog of Unabashed Gratitude* aloud to his friends. bell hooks' *All About Love*, J.M. Coetzee's *Slow Man*, Julio Cortázar's short stories, and Camonghne Felix's *Yolk* are the new (to him) works he's currently reading.

KATIE FOWLEY: I am currently reading *The Art of Loving* by Erich Fromm, *Lowly* by Alan Felsenthal, and *Of Being Dispersed* by Simone White. Before bed, I dream-read Bruno Schulz's *The Street of Crocodiles* until I fall asleep. I have been reading *Paradise Lost* out loud with my girlfriend over the past three years, mostly on camping trips. I am also rereading some beloved books with my high school students, including Elena Ferrante's *My Brilliant Friend*, Claudia Rankine's *Citizen*, Carson McCullers' *The Member of the Wedding*, and Shakespeare's *The Tempest*. I am excited to read Adrienne Raphel's new book *What Was It For* and Dan Poppick's *The Police*.

YANARA FRIEDLAND is a German-American writer and teacher. Author of the novel *Uncountry: A Mythology*, she has been deeply inspired by the works of Clarice Lispector, Unica Zürn, and Thereska Hak Kyung Cha. She is currently reading Solmaz Sharif's *Look*, Eduard Glissant's *Poetics of Relation* and Hans Hildebrandt's *Die Frau als Künstlerin*.

CARMEN GIMENÉZ SMITH: *Sad Girl Poems* by Christopher Soto; *Incidents Of Travel In Poetry* by Frank Lima; *This Blue Novel* by Valerie Mejer; *Formol* by Carla Falser; *Asco: Elite Of The Obscure: A Retrospective 1972-1987* edited by C. Ondine Chavoya and Rita Gonzalez; *Kloaka: Una Antologia* published by Amagord Ediciones.

DAVID GREENWOOD says: I'm reading my favorite book, Robert Walser's *The Robber*. Most days I read some Henri Michaux or Kenneth Koch. John Rowe's gorgeous audio recordings of the first two volumes of Proust (sadly another dude reads the rest—I must kidnap John Rowe), and Jonathan Cecil's and Nigel Lambert's P.G. Wodehouse keep me on earth. A favorite novel of recent years is Bill Peters's *Maverick Jetpants in the City of Quality*.

RAQUEL GUTIÉRREZ: *Loving in the War Years: Lo Que Nunca Paso Por Sus Labios* (Cherríe L. Moraga); *The Ghost In Us Was Multiplying* (Brent Armendinger, Noemi Press); *The Possibilities of Mud* (Joe Jímenez, Korima Press); *Advice for Lovers* (Julian Talamantez Brolaski, City Lights).

TOM HAVIV: I'm reading Martin Buber's *Ten Rungs*.

NOY HOLLAND: These days I'm reading a lot of non-fiction of various stripes. Naomi Klein's *This Changes Everything*; Zach Savich's *Diving Makes the Water Deep*; and Hilary Plum's stunning *Watchfires*.

DAVID HOLLANDER: I recently read the new DeLillo, *Zero K.* For a while it seemed so humorless as to border on parody, but the final third was crushingly good. I tackled the first of the Knausgaard books that everyone's been pushing on me for months. Strange experience. I was somehow both deeply invested in K.'s Way of Seeing, and puzzled by the purposeful lack of narrative motion. I read Jenny Offill's *Dept. of Speculation* a few months back. Cool (and sad) book that seems to represent the 21st century novelist's burgeoning embrace of fragmentation. Currently re-reading John Hawkes' *The Lime Twig* (which is as haunting and anxiety-provoking as I remember). Next up is German author Jenny Erpenbeck's *The End of Days*.

FLORENCE KINDEL: The poets I am reading now are Lorine Niedecker, Bernadette Mayer and Gertrude Stein. I am also inspired by the study of physics, which I find has a close to connection to the creative arts.

KATHRYN MARIS: British poetry is in a thrilling phase. Two essential print magazines are *Poetry London* and *The Poetry Review*. Three online journals I recommend are *Poems in Which*, *Prac-Crit* and *tender*. The new Penguin Modern Poets series, re-lauched last year, offers intergenerational and transatlantic groupings of exciting contemporary poets. The DIY scene is also thriving: my favourite alternative presses are Swimmers, Test Centre, Clinic, and If A Leaf Falls (which emphasizes appropriative and arbitrary writing practices)."

JASON MITCHELL: Currently reading Alli Warren's *I Love It Though*, Brian Walters' translation of Lucan's *Civil War*, and Aimé Césaire's *The Collected Poetry* translated by Annette J. Smith and Clayton Eschleman. A few recent favorites: Jai Arun Ravine's *The Romance of Siam*, *Opening Day* by George Stanley, *Tripwire 12*, Arlo Quint's *Wires and Lights*, and *Valve* by Katie Fuller.

RUSTY MORRISON: The two books that I'm carrying around with me this week, which means I'm actively reading them: Renee Gladman's *Ana Patova Crosses a Bridge* (there's no one like Renee Gladman. She defies descriptors) and *Inhuman Nature* edited by Jeffrey Jerome Cohen, which has footnotes that've led me to buy Jane Bennett's *Vibrant Matter* and Tim Ingold's *Being Alive: Essays On Movement, Knowledge, Description*. But I've not started either of those. In the evening, this week, I'm reading Sarah Bakewell's *At The Existentialist Cafe: Freedom, Being, and Apricot Cocktails*.

VALÉRIE MRÉJEN has been reading a lot of Stefan Zweig.

NICHOLAS D. NACE: In today's mail came Charles Altieri's *Reckoning with the Imagination: Wittgenstein and the Aesthetics of Literary Experience* (Cornell, 2015), Rachel Zolf's *Janey's Arcadia* (Coach House, 2014), Craig Dworkin's *Alkali* (Counterpath, 2015), and a periodical that my local electric company publishes. But at the top of the yet-to-be-read stack are James Wood's *The Nearest Thing to Life* (Brandeis, 2015) and Helen Vendler's *The Ocean, the Bird, and the Scholar* (Harvard, 2015). That said, the remainder of the day will be spent with Walter Scott's *Lay of the Last Minstrel* (Ballantyne, 1805).

URAYOÁN NOEL: On my desk now are Aracelis Girmay's *The Black Maria* (2016) and Haitian writer Frankétienne's *Chaophonie* (2014). Two reissues I'm exploring are Companhia das Letras's 2016 edition of Brazilian poet Ana Cristina César's *A Teus Pés* (1982) and Folium's 2016 edition of Puerto Rican poets Ángela María Dávila and José María Lima's *Homenaje al ombligo* (1966). On the critical/activist front, I'm enjoying Sunaura Taylor's *Beasts of Burden: Animal and Disability Liberation* (2017) as well as Javier E. Laureano's *San Juan Gay* (2016). For some reason, I'm also attempting to translate Stephen Jonas into Spanish.

KELLI ANNE NOFTLE: *The Mother of All Questions*, Rebecca Solnit; *Proxies*, Brian Blanchfield; *Falwell: An Autobiography*, Jerry Falwell.

CALEB NOLEN: Currently I am reading the poetry of Gerard Manley Hopkins and Lucille Clifton. I am also reading Hans Urs von Balthasar's *Dare We Hope 'That All Shall Be Saved'?*, and *Species Beings and Other Stories* by Frére Dupont.

ALIX ANNE SHAW: Jay Besemer, *Chelate*, from Brooklyn Arts Press. Julia Cohen, *Triggermoon*, *Triggermoon* from Black Lawrence, *Night Sky with Exit Wounds*, Ocean Vuong, Copper Canyon, and Deleuze and Guattari, *A Thousand Plateaus*.

BUZZ SLUTZKY: I recently discovered *Weird Fucks* by Lynne Tillman from *The Soho Press Book of 80s Short Fiction* after finding the book in a free box down the street; I get the sense that my ancestors sent it to me for a higher purpose. Other books swimming around in my fiction mind include Leopoldine Core's *When Watched*, Sarah Schulman's *After Delores*, and that book's lesbian thriller ancestor *The Price of Salt*, by Patricia Highsmith. Next on my reading list are *Small Beauty* by jia qing wilson-yang and, after seeing her perform, I am desperate to read anything by Pamela Sneed.

WILL SMILEY is reading *Scyld & Scef* and *Everyday Life in Viking-Age Towns*.

CHRIS STROFFOLINO: My favorite new books of 2016 are/were *Stamped from the Beginning* (The Definitive History of Racist Ideas) by Ibram X. Kendi, *De-Facto Feminism* by Judy Juanita, and *Olio* by Tyehimba Jess.

JULIA TILLINGHAST'S Recommended Reading: *Fire Water World Among the Dog Eaters*, by Adrian C. Louis, Tracy K. Smith's first book, *The Body's Question, Anybody*, by Ari Banias, Philip Metres' *The Sand Opera*, Emily Toder's *Beachy Head*, and Bob Hicok's *Love & Sex &*.

EDWIN TORRES: I'm putting together an anthology and discovered this book by a speech therapist which has thrown me for a loop. *Mary Stuart's Ravishment Descending Time* by Georgiana Peacher, published in 1992 is an extraordinary Joycean journey beyond description. That's just the tip of what's rocking my boat these days.

JASMINE DREAME WAGNER: Lauren Berlant's "'68, or Something," Donna Haraway's "A Cyborg Manifesto," Wayne Koestenbaum's *My 1980s*, Maggie Nelson's *The Art of Cruelty*, Masha Tupitsyn's *Beauty Talk & Monsters*, Christine Shan Shan Hou's *Food Cuts Short Cuts*, and anything that catches my eye on Facebook, Twitter, and Tumblr.

M. WEST: I am re-reading *The Summer Book*, by Tove Jansson, just finished *Hyperbole and a Half*, by Allie Brosh, am reading the second volume of *Harry Potter* out loud to my children and reading about the chemistry and machinery involved in nephrology nursing.

HAZEL WHITE: *Ban en Banlieue*, by Bhanu Kapil; *The Forever War*, by Dexter Filkins; *Missing the Moon*, by Bin Ramke; *Place*, by Tacita Dean and Jeremy Millar; *The Racial Imaginary: Writers on Race in the Life of the Mind*, edited by Claudia Rankine, Beth Loffreda, and Max King Cap.

FE
NC
ED